THE HERITAGE OF INDIA SERIES (9)

CLASSICAL SANSKRIT LITERATURE

THE HERITAGE OF INDIA SERIES (9)

CLASSICAL SANSKRIT LITERATURE

BY

A. BERRIEDALE KEITH, D.C.L., D. Litt.

GYAN

Published by

Gyan Publishing House
5, Ansari Road
Daryaganj, New Delhi-110002
Phone: 011-47034999, 9811692060
E-mail: books@gyanbooks.com

Distribution Network
gyanbooks.com
India, USA, Canada, UK, Australia, France

ISBN: 978 81-212-8269-7 (PB)
First Published, 1923

2nd Impression 2023

Printed at: Gyan Press, Delhi.

THE HERITAGE OF INDIA SERIES (9); CLASSICAL SANSKRIT LITERATURE
Author: A. BERRIEDALE KEITH

THE HERITAGE OF INDIA SERIES

CLASSICAL SANSKRIT LITERATURE

BY

A. BERRIEDALE KEITH, D.C.L., D.Litt.

OF THE INNER TEMPLE, BARRISTER-AT-LAW, AND OF THE SCOTTISH BAR,
REGIUS PROFESSOR OF SANSKRIT AND COMPARATIVE PHILOLOGY
AT THE UNIVERSITY OF EDINBURGH.
AUTHOR OF 'SANSKRIT DRAMA,' ETC.

PREFACE

To sketch the history of Classical Sanskrit Literature within the limits of a volume of the Heritage Series would have been impossible but for the decision to allot another volume to the Sanskrit Drama, in which the literature of India attains its highest perfection. It has seemed best also to restrict this review to the period before A.D. 1200, a date conventional indeed, but yet late enough to include all the great masterpieces of Sanskrit literature. Even within the limit chosen attention has been concentrated on the works of chief merit or reputation, and it has been necessary to avoid any detailed discussion of controversial dates, in order to dwell upon the substance and form of the literature itself. Here again it has only been possible to indicate in outline the salient features of the classical literature, and to suggest some of the many problems affecting its origin and development. The aim of this work will be accomplished if it serves to remind readers of the richness and variety of the literature of which it treats, and encourages students to extend the field of their reading in Sanskrit.

The literary judgments expressed are based on the assumption that classical Sanskrit literature is entitled to rank among the great literatures of the world, and that therefore it must be subjected to the same standards as are applied to them. Analogous standards in effect must have influenced the judges of poetry in mediæval India, for they accord in acclaiming as the first of Sanskrit poets Kālidāsa, to whom Western critics without hesitation assign the same rank.

Edinburgh, A. BERRIEDALE KEITH.

January, 1923.

PREFACE TO SECOND EDITION

A REPRINT of this sketch having become necessary, the opportunity has been taken to make a few verbal changes and to add some references to recent works.

The question of the date of dramas ascribed to Bhāsa by the late T. Gaṇapati Śāstrī, whose death inflicts a grave loss on Indian scholarship, affects so closely certain matters dealt with in this book that I should, perhaps, state briefly the reasons which render me satisfied that his identification of the author is correct. I hold it as conclusively established that the author of the *Cārudatta* was earlier than the *Mṛcchakaṭikā*; that all or almost all the Trivandrum plays are by the same author; and that this author ranks higher than any Sanskrit dramatist other than Kālidāsa. Whether we give a name to this dramatist is indeed a minor matter; but, when we find that pre-eminent among the plays is the *Svapnavāsavadattā*, and that ancient critics who had before them Bhāsa's dramatic output ranked his *Svapnavāsavadattā* as supreme, it seems idle to refuse to accept Bhāsa's authorship. How far the plays as we have them represent Bhāsa's own version is a problem as little soluble as the question of the original form of the *Śakuntalā* of Kālidāsa; none the less the genius of both authors is equally undeniable. On this point I am happy to find recent confirmation in an article in the *Festgabe Jacobi* by an author of high artistic sensibility, H. Weller, who demonstrates the affinity in style and spirit of certain of the verses ascribed to Bhāsa in the anthologies with passages in the Trivandrum plays. Nor can I find in the vast literature on the subject a single satisfactory argument to prove that the dramas, by reason of technique, metre, Sanskrit, or Prākrit, are later than those of Kālidāsa, who, it seems to me as to T. Gaṇapati Śāstrī, knew the plays as those of the great predecessor with whose fame he had to contend in his youth.

The University of Edinburgh,
May, 1927.

A. BERRIEDALE KEITH.

CONTENTS

		Page
I.	Classical Sanskrit	7
II.	The Predecessors of Kālidāsa	21
III.	Kālidāsa	29
IV.	Post-Kālidāsan Epic	46
V.	Historical Kāvya	57
VI.	The Prose Romance and the Campū ...	66
VII.	The Popular Tale	84
VIII.	The Didactic Fable	96
IX.	Lyric and Gnomic Verse	107
X.	Theories of Poetry	121
	Index	137

I

CLASSICAL SANSKRIT

It is characteristic of the paucity of our information of the early history of Sanskrit literature that a serious controversy has arisen as to the language in which secular literature was first composed. It has been suggested, with more or less clearness, that for profane as opposed to sacred literature Sanskrit was originally not employed. It was essentially in the form in which it was regulated by the grammar of Pāṇini, in the fourth century B.C., a form of speech reserved for those who conducted sacrifices and engaged in theological speculation, in effect for the Brahmins. Other persons used a true vernacular, which may be described as Primary Prākrit, in order to distinguish it from the Prākrits which have been preserved in the grammarians and in literature, and which represent a chronologically later stage of speech. It was in some Primary Prākrit that secular literature was first composed, and it was only late that the sacred language was extended to the meaner use, perhaps as Professor Lévi has suggested,[1] through the initiative of the Śaka Satraps of Western India in the course of the second century A.D., one of whom, Rudradāman, is responsible for the first official inscription in Sanskrit throughout, and whose official nomenclature seems to be reflected in the rules for the use of titles in the Sanskrit drama laid down in the *Bhāratīya Nāṭyaśāstra*. The epics themselves, it has been suggested,[2] were long current in Prākrit before they were rendered, perhaps shortly after the Christian era, into Sanskrit. The motives for such translations and the impetus to compose in Sanskrit in lieu of

[1] *Ind. Ant.*, xxxiii, 163 ff. Contrast Keith, *Sanskrit Drama*, pp. 69 ff.

[2] *Ind. Ant.*, xxiii, 52. Contrast Keith, *J.R.A.S.*, 1914, pp. 1021 ff.; 1915, pp. 328 ff., 799 f.

Prākrit can easily be imagined; the culture of the Brahmins was becoming more and more the chief common possession of India, and the sacred language presented the only possibility of a speech which could claim comprehension readily throughout the vast area subject to Brahmanical influence. Further, during the period before and after the Christian era India was subject to invasion from the north-west and west and to considerable movements of population, which must have excited rapid changes of speech forms in the areas affected, and have driven poets and others, desirous of producing work to endure, to seek a medium more satisfactory than a vernacular in process of rapid alteration.

The theory has the attractiveness of simplicity, but the complexity of facts rarely admits of such easy solutions. We must recognise the scantiness of our information regarding the early speeches of India, the vast areas concerned, and the distinction of tribes and of classes within tribes. The Vedic language as we find it in the *Ṛgveda* and in the later Saṁhitās is already a poetical and hieratic language, which was doubtless different even from the speech of the priests in ordinary life and still further removed from that of the ruling and subject classes, not to mention the slaves or aborigines. The language of the Brāhmaṇas, the Āraṇyakas, and the Upaniṣads is equally a hieratic speech; it represents the language used by the priests primarily at the sacrifice, then in speculations based on the sacrifice, and extending ultimately beyond its immediate limits, not the language of everyday conversation either among the priests themselves or in intercourse with others.[1] It is undoubtedly a genuine continuation of the language of the Saṁhitās in so far as it is descended from the prose of the Saṁhitā period; indeed, while we have no prose as old as the *Ṛgveda*, there is no reason to doubt that the prose of the Saṁhitās of the *Black Yajurveda* is contemporaneous with the later verses of these texts. In the grammar of Pāṇini we find the norm laid down for the spoken language, Bhāṣā, of his time in the higher circles of society, a fact which explains the failure of the norm of Pāṇini to conform precisely to any texts which are preserved to us, though it has obvious

[1] See H. Jacobi, *Scientia*, xiv, 251 ff.; Patañjali on i, 1, 1, v. 9; i, 3, 1. Cf. H. Oldenberg, *Das Mahābhārata*, pp. 129 ff.

affinities with the language of such Brāhmaṇas as the *Aitareya*. The Bhāṣā shows little phonetic variation from the hieratic language, and we must recognise in this fact the dominant influence of the religious factor in stereotyping speech. We have of this a brilliant example in a quotation from an earlier authority preserved in Patañjali about 150 B.C. There were, we learn, at one time seers of vast knowledge, who, in their ordinary conversation, used incorrect expressions; thus for the correct *yad vā nas tad vā naḥ*, which denotes, 'We are content with our lot,' they said, *yar vā ṇas tar vā ṇaḥ*, but while sacrificing they strictly followed the correct forms. An expiatory sacrifice, the Sarasvatī, is also prescribed for any incorrect use of language in the sacrifice, and, when it is remembered how long the sacrifice might last, it is not surprising that the hieratic language exercised a most powerful stabilising effect on the language of the priests.

That in other circles and places there was a rapid change of language we may *a priori* readily admit, and the probability is confirmed by occasional traces in the Vedic language[1] itself of forms which show phonetic changes foreign to that type of speech. In this connection we must remember that, while the earliest Vedic hymns were composed in the Panjab, others belong rather to the region of Kurukṣetra, which is also the home of the great Brāhmaṇas, while the *Atharvaveda* in part may have its origin among tribes still further east, settled on the Ganges itself. The Brahmanical civilisation doubtless centered in the region of Kurukṣetra or the middle country, especially among the Kuru-Pañcālas,[2] but it spread beyond these limits to the land of the Kosalas and Videhas as well as to even more remote regions. It would be absurd to assume that the rate of linguistic change was uniform in the different localities; the communities must have been very varied in composition, some more affected than others by mixture with the aborigines, and therefore in all probability likely to alter more rapidly their speech. This factor of race mixture must have played an important part in the creation

[1] How far these are original, how far substituted in transmission, is insoluble.

[2] Macdonell and Keith, *Vedic Index*, i, 165 ff.

of the Prākrits, not, of course, in the sense that these represent the treatment of Vedic by aborigines,[1] whether Dravidian[2] or Austro-Asiatic[3] in speech, on whom it was forced by their masters, but as influencing the racial character and speech capacity and habits of the Aryan tribes.

These facts, however, leave us entirely without information as to the language in which secular literature was composed before or contemporary with Pāṇini. Nor are we carried any further by the fact that both the Buddha and Mahāvīra, the founder or renovator of Jainism, in the fifth century B.C. used some form of Prākrit, possibly the precursor of Ardha-Māgadhī; those were rival religions to Brahmanism, and moreover flourished primarily in regions which were outside the plane of Brahmanism proper. How far this Prākrit differed from the Bhāṣā of Pāṇini we have no means of saying, for neither the Pāli nor the Jain Prākrit has any serious pretension to represent the speech of the Buddha or Mahāvīra. It is more important that in the inscriptions of Aśoka in the second half of the third century B.C. and in epigraphical records generally until the second century A.D. we find Prākrits, and not Sanskrit. As far as a Buddhist Emperor was concerned anything else was out of the question, and the influence of the Empire doubtless affected all its successors. But we need not doubt that some form of Prākrit appealed more directly and easily than Sanskrit to the comprehension of the generality of the subjects of the Aśokan Empire and in the subsequent period.[4] We must note, however, that the Aśokan edicts show us the attempt to establish the language of the capital as a *lingua franca* in lieu of Sanskrit, an effort which was clearly doomed to failure, so inferior is the Prākrit to Sanskrit as a means of expression.

It is upon this epigraphical use of Prākrit that the belief that secular literature was composed originally in Prākrit essentially depends. Yet the argument is clearly without cogency; it conceives a priesthood devoted to Sanskrit on the one hand, a secular population equally devoted to Prākrit on

[1] Cf. Keith, *Cambridge History of India*, i, 109 f.

[2] Cf. S. K. Chatterji, *Bengali Language*, i, 40 ff., 170 ff., with J. Bloch, *Bull. Soc. Ling.*, 1924, pp. 10 ff.

[3] Cf. J. Przyluski, *Journal Asiatique*, ccviii, 1 ff., 53 f.

[4] On Pāli cf. Keith, *Ind. Hist. Quarterly*, i, 501 ff.

the other, making no allowance for the complex gradation of Indian society which can be traced clearly in the later Saṁhitās and is visible in large degree even in the *Ṛgveda* itself. That a popular secular literature in Prākrit such as the folk tale existed, we need not doubt, but we have every reason to believe that there existed a more aristocratic literature in Sanskrit, not indeed in the Bhāṣā of Pāṇini, but in a form of speech closely allied to it, current among the rhapsodes and their patrons. Of this literature we have a monument in the *Rāmāyaṇa* and the *Mahābhārata*, neither of which is in any sense a product of, though loved by, the populace. The nearest parallel to these works is to be found in the aristocratic literature of Greece, the *Iliad* and the *Odyssey*, the fine flower not of village life, but of the Courts of the great princes of the Ægean. The priesthood formed, as in Egypt, a vital part of this high culture and made the epics largely their own,[1] but the language is not that of the hieratic speech. It is freer, less archaic, more inaccurate, simpler, less fine an instrument of expression no doubt, but more practical. It possesses a distinctive idiosyncracy of its own which renders ludicrous the suggestion that it is turning into the hieratic speech of some Prākrit; we have in the so-called Gāthā literature of Buddhism genuine examples of the result of the process of transformation, which are miles apart from the epic speech. That Pāṇini ignores the language of the epic is no proof that it is younger than his date; his work is not a disquisition on Sanskrit, but a manual of practical rules regulating the correct speech of the priesthood as the highest form of expression, and it in no wise falls to him to take account of less elevated forms of language. The epics again ignore the rules of Pāṇini in their finer nuances, simply because they represent the language of classes who did not aim at the linguistic perfection of hieratic circles.

Apart from the question of language, there is now abundant evidence to show that the epics existed in some form in Sanskrit before Pāṇini, and that the idea of translation about the Christian era is wholly untenable. Apart from the absolute silence of history on so portentous an undertaking, it is plain

[1] See H. Jacobi, *Gött. Gel. Anz.*, 1899, p. 880; H. Oldenberg, *Das Mahābhārata*, p. 14.

that there existed no conceivable ground for such action at the period in question, which was one of the comparative eclipse of Brahmanism and of the domination of foreign influences. But, if the epics were composed in Sanskrit, the originality of the classical literature is assured, for from the epic a direct development leads to the Kāvya, which is the highest form of the classical literature apart fron the drama. There is a very real sense in which the *Rāmāyaṇa* can be said to be the first Kāvya; though it has been embellished in the course of redaction, it is impossible to deny to Vālmīki the command of a literary art[1] which rendered the tendency to embellish a natural complement of his work, and not the introduction of an alien style. The elegance of Vālmīki's handling of metre and his skilled use of figures of speech are precursors of the daintiness and polish of Kālidāsa.

How wide was the circle to which the epic could appeal in Pāṇini's time[2] we do not know, but we have a couple of centuries later the evidence of Patañjali as to the speech of his day. From him we learn that the norm of speech in his day were the Śiṣṭas, the learned Brahmins of Āryāvarta, who, whether they studied grammar or not, had a hereditary skill in the correct use of the tongue and from whose employment of it others could acquire it. Others, however, were less precise in speech; thus they mispronounced sounds, making *ṣaṣa* of *śaśa*, *palāṣa* of *palāśa*, and *mañjaka* for *mañcaka*. Again they used incorrect terms (*apaśabda*), mainly nouns, often in Prākrit forms adapted slightly to seem Sanskrit, more rarely in verbal forms, a graver deviation. We have in the *Rāmāyaṇa* a similar distinction drawn between the correct speech of the Brahmin and the less precise language of an ordinary man who uses Sanskrit.[3] In Patañjali we have the well-known anecdote of the grammarian and the charioteer who dispute over the etymology of the latter's title, Sūta, and the correctness of the formation of the word *prājitṛ*, driver. The same author contemplates the use of Sanskrit in ordinary life (*loke*) just as Prākrit is used, and Pāṇini himself gives words dealing with dicing and from the speech of herdsmen.

[1] H. Jacobi, *Das Rāmāyaṇa*, pp. 119 ff.; O. Walter, *Indica*, iii, 11 ff.

[2] A date about 350 B.C. agrees best with Pāṇini's position in the literature.

[3] H. Jacobi, *Das Rāmāyaṇa*, p. 115.

A very important light on usage is thrown by the practice of the drama, now attested for the first or second century A.D. by the fragments of Aśvaghoṣa, in which the higher characters, persons of cultivation and education of the Brahmin and ruling classes, speak Sanskrit, while women and men of lower rank normally speak Prākrit. To suppose that this is a convention without derivation from real life,[1] and owing its origin to the introduction of Sanskrit into an originally Prākrit drama, is a wholly implausible conjecture, for the drama, as we know, is essentially connected on the one hand at least with the dramatic recitation of epic material in Sanskrit,[2] and was doubtless in part at least in Sanskrit from its creation; Bhāsa,[3] it is interesting to note, has actually one epic drama without Prākrit, and there is little Prākrit in his short epic pieces. Nor can we believe that in early times at any rate the dramas were incomprehensible to the audience; the *Nāṭyaśāstra* expressly lays it down that the Sanskrit is to be such as to be easily intelligible by everyone. Moreover we have striking evidence in the dramas themselves of the aim at realism. The Prākrits of Aśvaghoṣa and Bhāsa differ markedly, the latter tending towards the norm of Kālidāsa. That dramatist again adds Māhārāṣṭrī to the Prākrits known by the older writers, for Māhārāṣṭrī by his day had attained vogue through its use in lyrics, and thus seemed fit for the stage lyrics placed in the mouths of those who in prose spoke the standard Śauraseni.

Patañjali, as we have seen, mentions dramatic recitations of epic type, including the story of the slaying of Kaṁsa by Kṛṣṇa and the binding of Bali by Viṣṇu and like Pāṇini he most clearly knows the Bharata epic. But it is clear also that other forms of literature of a secular character were well known by him.[4] We hear of rhapsodes who recite their stories until the day dawns, and of tellers of the tales of Yavakrīta, Priyaṅgu, Yayāti, Vāsavadattā and Sumanottarā

[1] S. Lévi, *Le Théâtre Indien*, i, 335.

[2] Cf. Keith, *Sanskrit Drama*, pp. 69 ff.

[3] See Keith, *Bulletin School Oriental Studies*, iii, 623 ff.; T. Gaṇapati Śāstrī, ibid., 627 ff.; G. Harihar Śāstrī, *Indian Historical Quarterly*, i, 370 ff.; H. Weller, *Festgabe Jacobi*, p. 125.

[4] Weber, *Ind. Stud.*, xiii, 356 ff., 477 ff.; Kielhorn, *Ind. Ant.*, xiv, 326 f.; Bhandarkar, *Ind. Ant.*, iii, 14.

as well as of Bhīmaratha. Significant is the citation and comment on a verse, 'He, at whose birth ten thousand cows were bestowed on the Brahmins who brought the joyous tidings, now lives on what he can glean, for it is explained that the term *priyākhya* is used by poetic licence (*chandovat kavayaḥ kurvanti*) for *priyākhyāya*. A *Vāraruca Kāvya*, or poem by Vararuci is mentioned. What is still more significant is the occurrence incidentally of verses in the ornate metres of the later Kāvya style. Thus we have examples of the Mālatī, Pramitākṣarā, Praharṣiṇī, and Vasantatilaka, as well as of simpler metres, such as the Śloka or the Triṣṭubh. Nor are the verses heroic only in subject matter; they are in some cases clearly erotic as in the fragment, 'O fair limbed one, the cocks unite to proclaim' ('*varatanu sampravadanti kukkuṭāḥ*'), which recurs later. We have evidence also that the didactic style was already known, as in 'Ambrosial, not deadly, are the blows teachers give to the young; to spoil them produces vice, reproof creates virtue.' References to proverbs, such as that of the goat and the razor (*ajākṛpāṇīya*) and the crow and the palm fruit (*kākatālīya*), as well as to the hereditary enmity of the snake and the ichneumon, crow and owl, and so forth, suggest that the beast fable was already a genus of literature. Patañjali, therefore, indicates the existence in some form or other of practically all the main branches of classical Sanskrit literature.

The influence of this Sanskrit literature is probably to be discerned in the very slight evidence of Prākrit Kāvya style, which we have for this century, in the shape of the two inscriptions of dubious interpretation in the Sītābengā and Jogīmārā caves on the Rāmgarh hill, and it is probable also that the inscription of Khāravela of Kaliṅga, which is often referred to this century, though others place it later, was influenced in its style, which differs manifestly from that of the Aśokan records, by the Sanskrit Kāvya.[1]

Conclusive proof of the vogue of Sanskrit for *belles lettres* is evinced by the epics of Aśvaghoṣa and his dramas in which

[1] Lüders, *Bruchstücke buddhistischer Dramen*, pp. 41 f., 62; Bloch, *Arch. Survey India Report*, 1903–04, pp. 128 ff.; Boyer, *Mélanges Lévi*, pp. 121–28.

he applies that language to popularise Buddhism itself. That he should have thought it desirable so to do is conclusive evidence of the vogue of the Kāvya and the drama. Moreover, the Prākrits of Aśyaghoṣa are of high importance, for they exhibit Prākrit at a stage anterior to the softening or disappearance of intervocalic mutes and to the setting in of lingualisation of the dental nasal. It is impossible now to maintain that the Māhārāṣṭrī lyric, which is preserved for us in the collection of stanzas under the name of Hāla and in later texts, is the prototype of the Sanskrit lyric. That existed, we may be certain, as early as the second century B.C., and doubtless before that date, while the Māhārāṣṭrī lyric was the outcome of study of Sanskrit models and its language, far from being a true vernacular, is a remarkable adaptation for purposes of song, in which the elision of consonants has been carried to a degree which would have rendered the language inadequate for purposes of intelligible speech.

Aśvaghoṣa's action was symptomatic of the end; the claim of Sanskrit to be the language *par excellence* for secular literature was now established, and its influence grew with the stereotyping of the Prākrits and their reduction to merely literary use which early set in, as is evinced by the fact that after Kālidāsa, at any rate, the Prākrit of the dramas is unchanging. Over these languages Sanskrit had the enormous advantage that it had a real life in the Brahmanical schools and was always in some measure employed among the upper classes in conversation, while many who could not venture to speak it understood it adequately. It was in pre-Muhammadan times essentially the language of culture. It was used, for instance, as we learn from the medical compilation which passes under the name of Caraka,[1] in discussions on medical topics, and in the Jain *Upamitibhavaprapañcakathā*, written in A.D. 906, Siddharṣi deliberately adopts Sanskrit as the language of his allegory of human life, because persons proud of their culture despise any other form of speech, and adds that his Sanskrit is simple so that it can be understood even by those who prefer Prākrit. Bhāmaha, about A.D. 700, in his treatise on rhetoric[2] contem-

[1] iii, 8.

[2] ii, 3. Cf. Bilhaṇa, xviii, 6. Cf. the use of Sanskrit in vernaculars by educated persons, attested by *Kāmaśāstra*, p. 60.

plates the production of Sanskrit poems which even women and children, of the upper classes, of course, can appreciate. The poetry was, we must recognise, essentially aristocratic; it was the product of men who enjoyed or sought the favour of princes such as Samudragupta, Harṣa, Yaśovarman, Bhoja, and Lakṣmaṇasena, and other great men, and we know from Bāṇa in the seventh, and Bilhaṇa in the eleventh century, how the poet wandered from little Court to Court seeking favour by the exhibition of his talent in composition, often extempore (*śīghrakavitā*). All the time inevitably the gulf between the literary language and the vernaculars was growing wider and wider, with the inevitable result that Sanskrit literature tended to increase in artificiality and lack of contact with real life.

The peculiar character of Sanskrit is illustrated by the absence of dialectical variations; we have, it is true, indications[1] in Yāska, Pāṇini, Kātyāyana and Patañjali of both eastern and northern speech variations as well as of special usages of the Surāṣṭras, Kambojas and of others, but these reflect a period anterior to the classical Sanskrit literature as we have it. That literature stands effectively under the control of Pāṇini and his followers, to whose rules it endeavours to make the tradition, inherited from the epic, comply as far as practicable. It was impossible for the poets entirely to banish irregularities from their works, but they certainly show proof of their anxiety to achieve this aim. Yet they deviate from the norm here and there in accordance with the epic; there are occasional cases of confusion of the active and the middle of the verb; of the gerund in *tvā* and that in *ya*; of the present participle active in *antī* and that in *atī*.[2] Kālidāsa among minor slips in grammar is responsible for the use of *āsa* in lieu of *babhūva*, and of *sarati* in place of *dhāvati*. Needless to say, other poets are not superior to the great master; all of them follow the epic in the free use of the perfect as a tense of narration, indifferent to Pāṇini's rule that it must be confined to things not experienced by one's

[1] Wackernagel, *Altind. Gramm.*, I, xliii.

[2] The forms *gṛhya* and *apasyatī* of the poet Pāṇini disprove his identity with the grammarian, despite Peterson, *Subhāṣitāvali*, pp. 54 ff. See also pp. 125, 126.

self. A vital distinction from the spirit of the Bhāṣā of Pāṇini and of the epic is the development of the nominal style, which manifests itself in diverse aspects. The use of a participle or participial derivative in lieu of a finite verb becomes normal; the use of a periphrasis of a noun with a verb of general denotation in lieu of a verb with specific sense is frequent; the construction of a sentence without any verb expressed grows in favour; of especial significance is the development of the use of compounds, often of considerable length, which take the place of subordinate clauses of every conceivable kind, and thus effect one essential aim of the classical poets, the compression of the greatest amount of meaning in the fewest words. Parallel with this development we find a steady deterioration in the delicate sense of language visible in Pāṇini; his subtle syntactical rules are often simply disregarded, or directly broken. Many forms recognised by him disappear, such as perfect participles in *āna*, the gerundive in *tavai*, the present formation *jajanti* from *jan*, the pronoun *tya*, adverbs in *trā*, a large number of nominal derivatives, the use of the verb *as* with derivatives in *ī* such as *śuklīsyāt*, and the interrogative *uta* in simple clauses of enquiry.

On the other hand we find the poets ready to exhibit in their works their intimate study of the grammarians by using forms which are isolated, and therefore evidently no longer in any sense living. Kālidāsa has the strange term *sausnātaka*, asking if one has bathed well, and the Avyayībhāva form, *anugiram*; this latter peculiarity is frequent in Bhāravi, and extremely common in various forms in Māgha, of whose style it is a definite note. Bhāravi inaugurates the practice of the use of the perfect middle as a passive with the subject in the instrumental, to be followed freely by Kumāradāsa and Māgha. Māgha distinguishes himself by his rarities; we find the idiom *mā jīvan*, let him not live; *khalu* with the gerund in the sense of prohibition; the gerund in *am*, which is only common in the Brāhmaṇa style; *klam*, be weary, as a finite verb, as in the *Bhaṭṭi-kāvya* and the *Kādambarī*; rare aorist forms; and the technical distinction between *vi-ṣvan*, eat noisily; and *vi-svan*, howl. Harṣa achieves the distinction of using the amazing form *darśayitāhe*, I shall show, based on a mistaken generalisation of the grammarians and unknown to earlier literature. The fondness for grammatical studies is attested by the love of the poets from Aśvaghoṣa onwards for similes from the field of grammatical studies, strange intruders as these may seem in verse. The complete assimilation of grammar is seen in those epics, which serve at once to display the author's capacity as a poet and to illustrate the rules of grammar, such as the *Bhaṭṭi-kāvya* in the seventh century A.D., Halāyudha's *Kavirahasya* in the tenth, and Bhīma or Bhauma's *Rāvaṇārjunīya* perhaps in the seventh.

The Sanskrit of the prose authors seems to be derived mainly from the same source as that of the poets;[1] it is true that some of them, such as Bāṇa and Daṇḍin, respect the rules of the grammar, and, besides using freely the aorist—which is rare save with certain verbs in the epic—employ correctly the perfect in narrative. But Subandhu ignores the restrictions regarding the perfect, and the greater precision of certain prose authors may be set down simply to the freedom from metrical difficulties which encouraged greater accuracy in the employment of forms. Nor is it possible to deny the close relationship between classical verse and prose, though the latter has the power of adopting more freely the creation of compounds.[2] An interesting inheritance of the prose, one not noted by the grammarians, is the rule by which the verb closes the clause, and the comparatively rigid word order, with which may be compared the practice of the hieratic prose of the Vedic period.

As was inevitable, classical Sanskrit was affected deeply by the contemporaneous existence of Prākrits beside it; while it has lost many of the roots and words recorded in the *Gaṇapāṭha* and the *Dhātupāṭha* attached to Pāṇini's grammar, it has appropriated many words from Prākrits. In some cases the Prākrit word is taken over practically unchanged, thanks to the possibility of regarding it as Sanskrit; thus it is probable that the term, *vicchitti*, which denotes in the language of poetics charm or elegance, is really a Prākrit form of *vikṣipti*, which was accepted as it seemed possible to regard it as derived from *vi-chid*, a derivation contradicted by the fact that *viccheda*, for instance, never has this meaning.

[1] Contrast H. Jacobi, *Das Rāmāyaṇa*, p. 118.
[2] Cf. the style of the Sūtras.

The curious *duruttara*, hard to overcome, of the Kāvya seems to be founded on Prākrit *duttara* for *duṣ-ṭara*, and Kṛṣṇa's style as Govinda may be really derived from Sanskrit *gopendra*. In other cases it is possible to see attempts to turn into correct Sanskrit Prākrit terms whose origin was misconceived; thus *māriṣa*, friend, seems no more than Prākrit *mārisa*, one like me; *rūkṣa*, tree is from *rukkha* from *vṛkṣa*;[1] *masṛṇa* from *masiṇa* for *mṛtsna*, soft; *nirbhara*, full, for *nibbhara*, of uncertain provenance. In the Sanskrit of the south words of Dravidian origin make their appearance undisguised save by formal Sanskritisation, and a cerebral *ḷ* is common. Dravidian loan words may be found also in the language of the north, whether taken from the local tribes or borrowed from the south. Other loan words are less common, such as the Iranian *divira*, writer, *bahādura*, as a title, or the numerous borrowings of Greek astronomical and astrological terms, such as Kālidāsa's *jāmitra*, in which it is rather hard at first to recognise the simple *diametron*.

Like the epic Sanskrit, classical Sanskrit ignores the accent, which is fully recognised by Pāṇini; in this it resembles Prākrit, for there is still very little evidence that the Vedic accent was preserved in the sources whence any Prākrit was derived. An interesting distinction between Pāli and classical Sanskrit lies in the fact that Pāli has practically lost the perfect while it has many traces of the aorist; the epic has the perfect but uses the aorist little, and the same rule applies to the classical language, save in so far as poets to display their learning, and still more freely some prose authors, employ the aorist.

In the stereotyping of its phonetics, at least in its written form, Sanskrit shows its essential divergence from Prākrit; the latter, literary as it was, remained sufficiently in touch with the progress of language to alter in the passing of time; we can see the development from Aśvaghoṣa through Bhāsa and the Prākrit of the *Nāṭyaśāstra* to Kālidāsa. But Prākrit also about the date of Kālidāsa became stereotyped, and for recognition of the changes of actual non-literary speech we must have resort to a third literary form of speech, the

[1] I agree with Oldenberg that *rukṣa* in *Ṛgveda*, vi, 3, 7, does not mean 'tree.'

Apabhraṁśa, which by A.D. 550 had already taken its place beside Sanskrit and Prākrit as one of the great literary forms. Apabhraṁśa is no popular dialect; it is Prākrit with an infusion from the popular speech (*deśabhāṣā*) of its flexion, pronouns and adverbs, with a limited amount of its vocabulary, but essentially in vocabulary Prākrit and influenced in other respects by Prākrit. To make a true vernacular into a literature is not the function of Apabhraṁśa, but to bring Prākrit more closely into contact with ordinary speech. It is of importance that, while Prākrit and Sanskrit agree essentially in spirit and structure, this is quite otherwise in the case of Apabhraṁśa.[1]

[1] H. Jacobi, *Bhavisattakaha*, pp. 53 ff. The date of the *Paümacariya* of Vimalasūri, said to be the first Kāvya in Jaina Māhārāṣṭrī, which shows traces of Apabhraṁśa, is dubious, probably not before A.D. 300, as Greek astrology is known (cf. Jacobi, pp. 59 ff.). Vernacular poetry is known to Bāṇa. Cf. also S. K. Chatterji, *Bengali Language*, i, 88 ff.

II

THE PREDECESSORS OF KĀLIDĀSA

We have seen that classical Sanskrit has its root in the epic, and that the incidental hints in Patañjali are sufficient to show that the Kāvya was already practised in his day. The metre of the later Kāvya bears testimony to the same fact; it is essentially a hardening and stereotyping of the forms which the epic presents in the process of development, with one important addition, the borrowing of the Āryā metre, in all likelihood from Prākrit literature. Our first substantial poems which exhibit the full development of classical Sanskrit are, curiously enough, works not of Brahmanical writers, but of a Buddhist, who, knowing the devotion of the world to the objects of sense and its need for salvation, thought fit to win men's minds to the search for truth by presenting the tenets of his faith in the attractive and seductive form of the Kāvya. That the choice of this form should be made is conclusive evidence of its vogue and popularity in the first century A.D., and doubtless earlier, for Aśvaghoṣa in all likelihood is to be reckoned a contemporary of Kaniṣka and assigned with him either to the end of the first, or the middle of the second, century A.D.[1]

Of Aśvaghoṣa's two epics the greater, and probably[2] the later in time, is the *Buddhacarita*, which in its original form of 28 cantos, as known from Chinese and Tibetan versions, must have been a complete account of the life of the

[1] *Cambridge History of India*, i, 483; *Acta Orientalia*, 1924, pp. 52 ff.

[2] Hultzsch, *Z.D.M.G.*, lxxii, 121. On his philosophy, see Keith, *Buddhist Philosophy*, Chap. XV. The epic was first ed. by E. B. Cowell, Oxford, 1893, and trs. *S.B.E.*, xlix. A new ed. is now needed. On its grammar cf. Sukumar Sen, *Indian Historical Quarterly*, ii, 657 ff.

Buddha, but of which we have only 13 cantos, with a supplement of four more by a writer of the nineteenth century, carrying the narrative down to the conversions effected at Benares. The essential importance of the poem is the deliberate art with which the chaotic narratives of the older sources are reduced to measure and form on the lines evidently already definitively fixed for the Kāvya. From the opening of the poem, with its description of the city, the king, and the queen, to the end of the text we are entirely in the world of the later Kāvya save in its religious aspect. To deny or minimise the influence of Aśvaghoṣa on Kālidāsa is idle;[1] the exit of the young prince from the city brings the women to the windows and tops of the houses to gaze on his beauty, a passage (III, 13–24) which evokes the rivalry of Kālidāsa's description of Aja's entry in the *Raghuvaṁśa* (VII, 5–12). The prince, pursuing his way, beholds the hateful work of age and enquires the meaning, to be told by his charioteer the sad truth:

> It is age that has broken him; age, the robber of beauty, destroyer of strength, source of sorrow, ender of joy, the foe of the senses, the ruin of memory. He also has sucked as a babe at his mother's breast and learned to walk in the course of time; gradually waxed he great and strong in his youth; gradually has age overtaken him.

The prince's eyes are opened; in vain do the ladies of the harem seek to enchant his senses. 'How foolish,' he says, 'is the man who sees his neighbour grow sick, and old, and dead, and yet remains of good cheer nor is shattered by fear, as, when a tree, bare of flower or fruit, falls or is broken, the trees around are heedless of its fate.' It is in vain that the family priest expounds to him from the textbooks of politics the maxims of kingly duty (IV, 62–82); the prince must save his soul, and in a scene imitated from the *Rāmāyaṇa* (V, 9–11) his resolution is strengthened by the spectacle of his harem sunk in sleep (V, 48–62). Epic influence of another kind reveals itself in canto XII, where the philosophy of Arāḍa Kālāma is set out in terms closely reminiscent of the style of the philosophical expositions of the Sāṁkhya-

[1] Contrast Hillebrandt, *Kālidāsa*, p. 160. Aśvaghoṣa's influence appears in the curious separation of the elements of the periphrastic perfect; *Buddhacarita*, ii, 19; vi, 58; vii, 9; *Raghuvaṁśa*, ix, 61; xiii, 36.

Yoga of the *Mahābhārata*. In canto XII the heroic element again appears, for the Buddha does successful battle, in true epic fashion, with the tempter Māra.

The *Saundarananda*[1] is equally in epic style and all its cantos are preserved. Even more than the *Buddhacarita* does it bring us into close contact with the world of the epic and the Kāvya. Canto I describes in full detail Kapilavāstu, canto II the king, and III the Tathāgata, the perfect Buddha. His half-brother, Nanda, is dearly in love with his wife: 'Had Nanda not won Sundarī, or had not the lady with bent brows loved him, this pair would assuredly have been incomplete and lost their radiance, even as the night and the moon when severed.' Despite his wife's entreaties, Nanda is converted to the life of a monk, and Sundarī bitterly laments his defection (IV–VI). Nanda himself repents, and in a long list of historic examples asserts the overmastering power of love as justifying him in seeking reunion with his beloved (VII). Vainly are the demerits of women pointed out to him; 'there is honey on their lips, but deadly poison dwells in their hearts.' A journey to heaven is needed to convince him that the women of heaven are fairer far than his earthly love, and that his aim must be by penance on earth to attain the delights of the love of the Apsarases (X). But Ānanda proves to him, with abundance of mythological parallels, that the joys of heaven are not enduring; converted, Nanda seeks the Buddha, and receives from him full instruction in his doctrine (XII–XVIII).

Not only in spirit is Aśvaghoṣa a master of the Kāvya; he is ready to display his knowledge even of the more remote rules of grammar, such as the use in the *Saundarananda* of *asti* as a particle which is introduced into a simile (XII, 10), and in canto II he exhibits his skill in the use of a variety of aorists, although, like other Buddhist writers, he uses forms foreign to the classical style, such as *kim vata* or *prāg eva* as the equivalent of *kim uta*, and *saced* for *ced* or *maitrā* for *maitrī*. In the use of metres he shows in his epics, as in his dramas, much variety, including such rare forms as the Udgatā in canto III of the *Saundarananda*, as in Bhāravi (XXII) and Māgha (XV), the Suvadanā, and the Upasthita-

[1] Ed. Calcutta, 1910.

pracupita. Equal metrical skill is seen in his lyric *Gaṇḍīstotragāthā*, which describes the religious message conveyed by the sounds arising from the beating of a long piece of wood with a short club.

Unhappily, we have only in the form of a translation the *Sūtrālaṁkāra*,[1] in which, in prose and verse of the Kāvya style, is set out the substance of the Jātakas and Avadānas, which we find in the Pāli canon and in northern Buddhist records. The author mentions the *Buddhacarita* as well as the epics by name, and shows himself fully acquainted with the Brahmanical culture of the epics. The work, hitherto ascribed to Aśvaghoṣa, appears from fragments now published by Lüders to be by Kumāralāta.

The impression of the early bloom of the epic, as seen in Aśvaghoṣa, is confirmed by the evidence of the inscriptions.[2] The restoration of the Sudarśana lake, celebrated in the Girnar Praśasti of Rudradāman, refers to an event of A.D. 150 and dates from not much later. The language shows traces of incorrectness of the epic type as well as Prākrit influence, but it conforms admirably to the later rules of poetics in accumulating enormous compounds in the prose, in one case nine words of 23 syllables, in another 17 words of 40 syllables. Moreover, the sentences are of great length; one has over 23 Granthas of 32 syllables each. Of Śabdālaṁkāras, alliteration, either of the whole or parts of words or single letters, is frequent; of Arthālaṁkāras, figures of sense as opposed to sound, there are only the simile in two forms. But, what is far more significant, to the king is attributed skill in the composition of poems both in prose and verse (*gadyapadya*); even if the assertion be false, that is of no importance, for the essential point is that a king of an alien race, a Western Kṣatrapa, is conceived as likely to be interested in the elaborate poetry of the Kāvya style. Moreover, the description of the characteristics of such poems is significant, when compared with the qualities of the Vaidarbha style as set out in the early theorists; they are to be adorned by the qualities of simplicity, clearness, sweetness, variety,

[1] S. Lévi, *Journal Asiatique*, 1908, ii, 68 ff.; trs. Huber, Paris (1908); fragments ed. Lüders, Leipzig, (1926).

[2] F. Bühler, *Die indischen Inschriften und das Alter der indischen Kunstpoesie* (1890).

beauty and elevation through the use of poetic terminology, (*sphuṭalaghumadhuracitrakāntaśabdasamayodārālaṁkṛta*), terms which recall directly the possession of sweetness (*mādhurya*), beauty (*kānti*), and elevation (*udāratva*) of Daṇḍin's enumeration of the ten qualities of the Vaidarbha style.[1] Simplicity and clearness may well correspond to the Arthavyakti and Prasāda of the later enumeration, and variety may be compared with the force and strength (*ojas*) of expression later demanded. What is clear is that the poet of a Western Kṣatrapa Court was acquainted with rules of poetics and anxious to obey them. The same result may be attained from an examination of the Nāsik inscription of the nineteenth year of Siri Pulumāyi, the Siro-Polemaios of Baithana, Pratiṣṭhāna on the Godāvarī, of the geographer Ptolemy. The inscription is in Prākrit, but it shows clear traces of being produced by one who knew Sanskrit; indeed it may be no more than a deliberate turning into the official Prākrit of an original composed in Sanskrit. It is distinguished by the enormous compounds which fill its sentences, interrupted by short words to give the reciter a breathing space; it applies the ornaments of alliteration, and, unlike the Girnar Praśasti, alludes freely to the stock comparisons of the Kāvya; thus the king has might equal to that of Himavant, Meru and Mandara; his face is like the spotless lotus awakened from its sleep by the rays of the sun; his bravery is that of the heroes of the *Mahābhārata*, his glory that of the ancient kings of the epic; in his great feats, the demigods, the sun, the moon, and the planets share, just as in Bilhaṇa's historical epic Śiva intervenes to protect his favourite. Naturally the art here shown is far inferior to that of Subandhu or Bāṇa, but it is essentially of the same kind, and we find, as in Bāṇa, the deliberate insertion of brief phrases between masses of heavy compounds.

In a sense, a perfect example of the poetry of inscriptions produced under the influence of theory is afforded by the panegyric of Samudragupta by Hariṣeṇa, engraved on a pillar at Allahabad, some time probably before A.D. 350. It begins with eight stanzas, passes over to prose,[2] and ends with a

[1] See below, p. 124.

[2] Compare the Campū style, below, chap. vi. It is possible that Kālidāsa was influenced in his Digvijaya of Raghu by this panegyric.

stanza, the whole forming an enormous sentence, devoted to extolling the king, in which unity is secured by the mingling of compounds with relative clauses. The prose shows the characteristic love for long compounds, one attaining 120 syllables, but the effect is improved by the great care to produce rhythmical variation of quantity. In the verse we find no less than four different elaborate metres; alliteration is scantily employed, but metaphors and similes are not rare, and we have one instance of the Śleṣa, or double entendre, so beloved of the later Kāvya, but little patronised by Kālidāsa as a master of the Vaidarbha style; the king is a 'hero unfathomable, the cause of the elevation of the good and destruction of the bad (and thus a counterpart) of the unfathomable absolute, which is the cause of the origin and the destruction of the world, and in which good and bad have their being (*sādhvasādhūdayapralayahetupuruṣasyācintyasya*).'

There is a brilliant picture of the fateful moment when Candragupta in his old age chose Samudragupta as his heir before his darbar:

> 'He is noble,' with these words he embraced him, tremors of joy betraying his emotion; he gazed on him with tear-filled eyes, following his every movement, and weighing his worth—the courtiers sighed in relief and gloomy were the faces of his kinsfolk—and said to him, 'Do thou protect all this earth.'

Samudragupta, we learn, was a poet himself whose title of king of poets (*kavirāja*)—later the style of poet laureate awarded to successful writers—was established by the composition of many poems worthy of imitation by the learned, who was master of a poetic style worthy of study, and who enriched by his efforts the spiritual treasures of the poets. A few years later, in A.D. 400, we have an inscription of Vīrasena, minister of Candragupta II, who boasts his poetic skill, whence we may fairly deduce that Candragupta, no less than his glorious father, was a patron of the muses.

To this period, before Kālidāsa, must be attributed the evolution of the lyric metres, which are recognised freely in the *Chandaḥsūtra*[1] of Piṅgala, a work unfortunately not to be dated with any certainty, but doubtless not as late as the epoch of the great classical writers. The names given to

[1] Ed. *Kāvyamālā*, No. 91, 1908.

these metres in many cases can best be explained as originally epithets of the fair maidens who formed their themes; the poet, who first evolved a new form, or who took up such a form and won fame in it, was not remembered by name, but the stanzas remained current, and a description chosen from a name in them attached itself to them. The necessity for the lyric poet to aim at variation of metrical effect, in view of the inevitable monotony of his theme, accounts effectively for the multitude of metres recorded in the *Chandaḥsūtra*; the epic poets, on the other hand, were naturally less creative; they preferred metres in which long series of stanzas could be written with ease, and aimed at metric variety chiefly at the close of each canto.[1]

To yet another branch of literature we may turn for confirmation of the early bloom of the Sanskrit Kāvya, the *Kāmaśāstra*[2] or *Kāmasūtra*, which is undoubtedly in some form or other older than Kālidāsa and than Aśvaghoṣa, though it would be unwise to dogmatise regarding the precise date of the text as handed down under Vātsyāyana's name,[3] which appears to belong to Western India. That work represents obviously, and by its own admission, only the fruit of a long study which enured to the profit of the poets of the day. The fact is interesting, because, as Weber[4] long ago pointed out, the remote origin of the erotic lyric is to be found in the *Atharvaveda*, just as that of the religious lyric may be sought in the *Ṛgveda*, and the Brāhmaṇas already prove that the Hindu conception and observation of female beauty was that accepted in later times. The fact is noteworthy, for it has been suggested that the ideal of beauty and of its description found in the Sanskrit romance is un-Indian and a sign of borrowing from the Greek romance.

The *Kāmaśāstra*[5] is also of importance, since it preserves to us the picture of the ancient prototype of the man about town (*nāgaraka*) whose tastes and habits so largely inspire the

[1] H. Jacobi, *Z.D.M.G.*, xxxviii, 615 f.

[2] Ed. Benares, 1912; trs. R. Schmidt (7th ed.), Berlin, 1922.

[3] H. Jacobi, *Sitzungsber. d. Preuss. Akademie*, 1911, pp. 959 ff., 973; H. Chakladar, *Vātsyāyana* (1921); *A.B.I.*, vii, 129 ff.; viii, 43 ff.

[4] *Ind. Stud.*, viii, 172 f.; v, 218 ff.

[5] Pp. 43, 45 ff.; 52 ff. 60. Cf. Keith, *Sanskrit Drama*, p. 284 f.; H. Chakladar, *A.M.S.J.V.*; III, i, 327 ff.

literature of the period, and who is as typical of it as is the priest or the philosopher of the literature of the Brāhmaṇas and Upaniṣads. He is the fine product of city life, who, if banished thence by misfortune or trouble of any kind, seeks to reproduce in the country the refinements of his former *milieu*. His couch is soft, pigments, perfumes, garlands, a lute, a cage of parrots, and, last but not least, a romance, find their place in his chamber. His garden boasts a summer house, a swing in a shady spot; his days are spent in pleasure of all kinds; the mysteries of his toilet take time; his parrots must be taught new phrases; there are ram and cock fights, plays, concerts, and ballets to be attended, or excursions to be made to the parks in the vicinity of the city to picnic in the groves. Ladies of the *demi-monde* play a great part in these delights; at their houses—whose splendours are depicted both in the *Bṛhatkathāślokasaṁgraha*[1] and in the *Mṛcchakaṭikā*[2]—gaiety prevails, in which due attention is made to artistic and poetic topics. He is essentially, like his friends and hangers-on, a man of culture, but he must avoid the pedantry of an exclusive use of Sanskrit in his talk as much as the laxity of the normal use of the vernacular. That there was much that was dilettante in such a society is obvious, but we need not doubt that there was much genuine culture; witness Cārudatta's brilliant description of the power of Rebhila's song in Act III of the *Mṛcchakaṭikā*. The prevailing love interest of the literature is explained by the circles in which it arose, and from which alone it could expect recognition. It is significant of the strength of their influence that we find in the sixth century the resources of the Kāvya style employed to embellish what should have been the scientific astrological treatises of Varāhamihira,[3] while six centuries later the mathematician Bhāskara, a man of no mean achievement in that severe science, presents in the *Līlāvatī* his algebraical theorems in the guise of problems set to a fair maiden, the terms of which are chosen from the bees and flowers and other objects familiar to the poets.[4]

[1] x, 60–163. [2] iv.

[3] See *Bṛhatsaṁhitā*, ed. H. Kern, *Bibl. Ind.*, 1864–65.

[4] See H. T. Colebrooke, *Algebra* (1817). So also Śrīdhara, a predecessor of Bhāskara, in his *Triśatī*.

III

KĀLIDĀSA

INDIAN tradition has left us with no trustworthy knowledge of its greatest poet; stories of ignorance, enlightened by divine favour, cannot blind us to the conclusive evidence displayed in the works preserved to us of elaborate training in all the learning available to a Brahmin student of the Gupta era, from the science of politics to astrology and the Kāmaśāstra.[1] Tradition also leaves us in tantalizing ignorance of his date; the fancy that takes him to Ceylon to perish at the hand of a courtesan and makes his friend, king Kumāradāsa, in his grief cause himself to be burned by his side, cannot be seriously treated as evidence of a synchrony with that writer, whose *Jānakīharaṇa* shows conclusive signs of indebtedness to Kālidāsa. We are left, then, to such suggestions of date as can be gathered from Kālidāsa's works, and their position in the literature. It cannot seriously be doubted that he was later than Aśvaghoṣa and the dramatist, Bhāsa certainly in my opinion, whose plays we owe to the energy of T. Gaṇapati Śāstrī; everything points to his flourishing in the time of Gupta glory; the allusion to the horse sacrifice in the *Mālavikāgnimitra* is almost inevitably to be explained as a reminiscence of the performance of that rite

[1] See A. Hillebrandt, *Kālidāsa* (1921); S. Konow, *Das indische Drama*, p. 60 f.; Keith, *J.R.A.S.*, 1901, pp. 578 ff.; 1909, pp. 433 ff. An earlier date for Kālidāsa is excluded by the fact that not only does he know Greek astrological terms, but he is later than Bhāsa, who cannot reasonably be placed before A.D. 300. Hoernle's argument for Yaśodharman as Kālidāsa's patron (*J.R.A.S.*, 1909, pp. 104 ff.), and Pathak's preference for *c.* A.D. 450 are implausible; they date Vasubandhu much too late; cf. Keith, *Indian Logic and Atomism*, p. 96; *Sanskrit Drama*, pp. 143 ff. D. R. Bhandarkar (*A.B.I.*, viii, 200 ff.) supports Hoernle's view, but ignores the Mandasor inscription, a vital piece of literary evidence.

by Samudragupta renewing the glories of the ancient regime. The Vikramāditya, therefore, with whom Kālidāsa is associated in tradition, seems most naturally to be taken as Candragupta II, whose reign may be placed between A.D. 380 and 413. With this accords the fact that a Mandasor inscription by Vatsabhaṭṭi of A.D. 472–73 manifestly uses the *Ṛtusaṁhāra* and *Meghadūta*. Nor, even if the latter poem contains in v. 14, as is alleged by some commentators,[1] an allusion to Dignāga, have we any assurance that the date of the Buddhist philosopher was later than A.D. 400. The reference to the conquest of the Huns by Raghu in his Digvijaya in the *Raghuvaṁśa* has tempted the suggestion that Kālidāsa must have lived after the victory of Skandagupta over the Huns, half a century later than the date suggested above. But the evidence is far from convincing; there is nothing to indicate any reference to reality in this account of the exploits of a king of long ago, and, if Kālidāsa had lived in the reign of Skandagupta, when the fortune of the royal house was evidently tottering to a fall, it would be difficult to understand the calm contentment with the established order which marks all his works. His evident affection for Ujjayinī suggests that he spent much of his time in that State, which was brought under Gupta rule by Candragupta himself.

It is to his dramas, above all to the *Sakuntalā*, the finest work in classical Sanskrit literature, that Kālidāsa owes his greatest renown, but in the lyric and epic also he takes the first place among Indian poets. A work of his youth is certainly the *Ṛtusaṁhāra*, which has paid the penalty of juvenility in condemnation by modern, though not ancient, opinion as the product of some other hand.[2] This view is plainly unsound, as was the former attempt to deny Kālidāsa the *Mālavikāgnimitra* because of its inferiority to his other dramas. It is clear that Vatsabhaṭṭi used the poem, and this shows it to be of ancient date. It is perfectly true that it falls short of the later poems in depth of poetic insight and feeling, but a comparison, for instance, of Tennyson's early poems with the product of his mature years,

[1] Not by Vallabhadeva, but by Dakṣiṇāvartanātha as well as Mallinātha. Cf. Randle, *Fragments from Diṅnāga*, p. 3.

[2] See Keith, *J.R.A.S.*, 1912, pp. 1066 ff.; 1913, pp. 410 ff.; Hillebrandt, *Kālidāsa*, pp. 66–68.

shows precisely the same fact. The comparison is apposite, for Tennyson is precisely a parallel to Kālidāsa; both are poets not so much of inspiration and genius as of perfect accomplishment based on a high degree of talent. The comparative simplicity of the poem explains at once why no early commentaries are known; why Mallinātha deemed it needless to interpret it when he dealt with the three great poems; and why the writers on poetics do not cite from it to illustrate their rules. When they wished to allude to a description of the seasons every consideration of commonsense dictated that they should refer to the *Raghuvaṁśa*, Kālidāsa's masterpiece, rather than to a youthful and less perfect production. On the other hand, the poem by reason of its lack of elaborate art appeals more strongly to modern taste. Each of the seasons is reviewed in detail, in the six cantos with 153 stanzas which make up the work. The salient features in nature which mark each are described in loving and graceful detail, and the season's meaning for lovers is explained. The glow of the summer sun is painful even to lovers, but they find consolation in the nights when the heart of the moon is filled with jealousy as it gazes on the loveliness of maidens, but this is the very time when the heart of the wanderer is burned by the fire of separation from his beloved. In the rains love is suggested by the wild streams which eagerly embrace the tottering trees on their banks as they rush madly to the ocean, and by the clouds filled with rain which bend down to kiss the rocks of the mountain peaks. The creepers of autumn are the fair arms of maidens whose white teeth, seen through their red lips, are like the jasmine revealed through the crimson Aśoka flowers. In winter the fate of the Priyaṅgu creeper, buffeted by the breeze, is that of the maiden severed from her lover; for her whose lover is beside her this is the season of seasons. In the cool season which preludes spring, a fire and the mild rays of the reviving sun are pleasant to lovers, who find the moonbeams cold and the light of the star pale. Spring brings the blossoms of the mango, which are the arrows to be shot from the bow of the god of love to pierce the hearts of maidens. No deep feeling, it is true, marks the poem, but it is distinguished by a profound sympathy with the life of nature and an admirable power of describing in pregnant brevity the aspects of Indian scenery and life.

Later, but earlier perhaps than the epics, is the *Meghadūta*, doubtless the best known of Kālidāsa's works after the *Śakuntalā*. It has been suggested that in this work as elsewhere Kālidāsa owes some measure of inspiration to Vālmīki: the longing of Rāma for the lost Sītā is parallel with that of the banished Yakṣa for his dearly-loved wife, and the description of the rainy season in Book IV, canto 28, of the *Rāmāyaṇa* may well have given hints to the author in composing the *Meghadūta*. The Yakṣa owes his severance from his dear one to neglect in his duty, which Kubera, his lord, has punished with a year of exile; this he spends at Rāmagiri, in Central India, not far from Nāgpur, where in the rainy season he beholds a cloud on its northward way, a sight which brings to him the idea[1] of sending to his sorrowful bride a message of consolation and hope. He bids the cloud follow its way over mount Āmrakūṭa, quenching its forest fires with its rains, across the Narmadā, beneath the Vindhyas, over the city of Vidiśā, the stream Vetravatī, Ujjayinī in Avanti, the holy Kurukṣetra, the Ganges and the mountains whence it springs, and finally attain its end at Alakā on mount Kailāsa. The city is described, and the home of the Yakṣa; the suppliant entreats the cloud to let its lightning play gently, as if it were the radiance of the fireflies, and to muffle its thunder that it may not awake his beloved rudely from a dream, in which perchance she is thinking of her husband. He describes her changed by her grief as is the lotus by the frost; anxious to sing for her loved one, she cannot remember the melody, and she counts with flowers the days of their parting. The cloud is to give her the message of her husband's devotion and the assurance of ultimate reunion, when in nights, brilliant with the moonlight of autumn, they shall enjoy the desire of their hearts, rendered the more precious by their separation.

We miss, it is true, in this poem, the nearest approximation in tone to the Greek elegy[2] in Sanskrit literature, a certain measure of reality through the divine character of the Yakṣa and his bride; their severance is but temporary, their reunion certain, and the grief of the hero seems thus to

[1] Cf. *Jātaka*, ii, 143.
[2] See Hudson-Williams, *Early Greek Elegy* (1926).

modern feeling less than manly, for to us, as to the greatest of Greek historians,[1] courage to endure what is sent by heaven appears the duty of man. Schiller, who in his *Maria Stuart* makes the captive queen bid the clouds as they fly south greet the land of her happy youth, uses the motif in more effective guise; the hapless queen is well aware that for her there is no more chance of seeing again the fair land of France, and her position evokes true pathos. But this artistic defect must not be exaggerated; the end of poetry, in the theory of the writers on theory, is to suggest, not express, emotion, and the poem, stripped of its setting, speaks to us in tones of unmistakable earnestness of the sorrows of parted lovers, the melancholy delight in remembrance, and the joyful hope of reunion. It may be that here Kālidāsa expresses emotions which he has experienced in his own life story; the question is insoluble, and it is enough that the poem is a masterpiece of the description of the deepest, yet most tender, affection, in which passion is purified and ennobled. The power of description of nature foreshadowed in the *Ṛtusaṁhāra* is here seen heightened and more brilliant, as a result of the human emotion which pervades the poem. It is significant of the development of Kālidāsa's skill that the metre chosen for the work is throughout the Mandākrāntā, with its four verses, each of seventeen syllables, making up the stanza, with cæsuras at the fourth and tenth syllables. A much ampler means of expression of a single thought is thus available than within the restricted limits of the Indravajrā and Vaṁśasthā, which make up more than half of the *Ṛtusaṁhāra*, yet at the same time a severe strain is imposed on the capacity of the poet, but one to which he shows himself equal.

The poem is already imitated by Vatsabhaṭṭi, and it produced a crop of feeble attempts, the earliest perhaps the *Pavanadūta* of Dhoyīka (twelfth century). More important for its textual tradition is the *Pārśvābhyudaya* of the Jain Jinasena in the eighth century A.D., for the author, adopting the principle of Samasyāpūraṇa, the building up of a stanza on the basis of a given verse, has managed to work the text of the *Meghadūta*, as he knew it in 120 verses, into his

[1] Thukydides, ii, 64, 2 (Perikles).

account of the Jain saint, Pārśvanātha. Vallabhadeva in the twelfth, Mallinātha in the fourteenth century give the poem as having 111 and 118 verses respectively, a sign of the possibility of interpolation even in so famous a poem, which is attested also by the various recensions of the dramas.[1]

Next in date is doubtless the *Kumārasambhava*, which in some manuscripts occupies no less than seventeen cantos, but more often is reduced to seven. There can be no doubt whatever of the late origin of cantos IX to XVII.[2] They must have been added by one who thought that the eight cantos did not fulfil the purpose of the work, since they end with the description of the joys of Śiva and Pārvatī in wedlock. He insists, therefore, on bringing Kumāra into the world, and in describing in full his victory over the demon, Tāraka, whose destruction affords the motive for his birth, thus exceeding the promise of the title much more than the actual poem falls short of it. Fortunately, the defects of taste of the new cantos are not the only evidence of their later date. While Kālidāsa after the *Ṛtusaṁhāra* carefully avoids the repetition of the same phrases, his follower shamelessly brings forward again and again a phrase which has caught his fancy, much as does Bhāsa in his dramas. He delights in the use of prepositional compounds, contrary to the manner of Kālidāsa but in keeping with later taste, as also in his use of the perfect middle as passive with subject in the instrumental. Kālidāsa shows in a high degree the power to use his complicated metres without filling them with meaningless or feeble words, but this poet light-heartedly slips in words like *sadyas* or *alam*, delights in prefixing *su* to every available phrase, and shows his ingenuity in coining long synonyms for his characters. The metrical evidence is equally decisive; the cæsura at the close of the first and third verses of the Śloka is always observed by Kālidāsa, in these cantos it is omitted five times, and the

[1] Cf. K. B. Pathak, 2nd ed. of the *Meghadūta* (1916); Hari Chand, *Kālidāsa*, p. 244. Dakṣiṇāvartanātha (*c.* A.D. 1200) has 110 verses. Vallabhadeva's date is given as the tenth century by Hultzsch, who holds that his apparent knowledge of Bilhaṇa is an interpolation; see his trs. of Māgha, p. 224, n. 2, and his ed. of the *Meghadūta* (1911).

[2] H. Jacobi, *Verhandl. des V. internat. Orientalisten Kongresses*, ii, 2, 133 ff.

same laxity occurs six times with Upajāti stanzas; in the latter, even when the cæsura is respected, it is often weak, that is, at the end of a portion of a compound, a licence almost unknown to Kālidāsa. Further, the writers on poetics and the commentators ignore these cantos. Their spuriousness is thus incontestable; from the frequent use of *anta* in the end of compounds, which he compares with the Marāṭhī locative suffix *āṁt*, Jacobi has conjectured that the author was a Marāṭha writer. The case is entirely different with canto VIII, which is often passed over in the manuscripts, avowedly sometimes because of its erotic character. It is known to the writers on poetics, and is full of the spirit and style of Kālidāsa. It does not, we must admit, bring the poem to an effective termination, and no explanation of this defect is obvious. Do all our copies go back to a manuscript on birchbark, whose last leaf, as often, was hopelessly injured? Was the poet deterred from writing more by the criticisms of his first audience, to whom, as to Mammaṭa and Viśvanātha, the depicting of the erotic play of the supreme deity was distasteful? The question cannot be answered; that Kālidāsa was cut off by death before completing it is implausible, for the *Raghuvaṁśa* has every sign of later date.[1]

The poem opens with a description of the Himālaya viewed not in its terrible aspect, but as the home of demigods and spirits who delight in amorous sports, in which the maidens are glad to replace by the clouds the garments they have laid aside in their frolics. In this environment grows up Pārvatī daughter of the mountain god, perfect in every limb, whom the prediction of the sage Nārada has already designed as spouse for the great god Śiva, who sits, sunk in the deepest asceticism, on the mountain top, while Pārvatī with her friends serves him in obedience to her father's command, plucking the flowers for the offerings to him and tending his altar. In canto II the gods, menaced by the demon Tāraka, appear in sad plight before Brahmā himself; they beg his aid, but he has extended his favour to Tāraka and he cannot break faith; the poison tree one has planted must not be cut down by the

[1] O. Walter's objections (*Indica*, iii, 14 f.) are clearly insufficient, though Pischel (*Die orientalischen Literaturen*, p. 201) shares the view that the *Raghuvaṁśa* is early.

author of its being.[1] To Śiva the gods must have recourse; Pārvatī's beauty must be the magnet to win him from his penance, for from their union shall be born he who alone can destroy the foe. Indra, accordingly, as king of the gods, goes to seek the aid of the love god, Kāma. In canto III Kāma gladly promises his aid, if he can have Spring as his companion; accompanied by his friend, whose advent makes all nature revive, and Rati, his true wife, he advances with his bow ready, but is abashed by the spectacle of the great ascetic, until at the sight of Pārvatī he recovers courage. But at the moment when he would discharge his dart, Śiva, who has felt an unwonted perturbation of heart, burns the luckless Kāma to ashes by the flame of anger proceeding from his eye. In canto IV Rati bewails her husband; to Spring, who seeks in vain to console her, she says: 'Once departed, thy friend will return no more, like the flame which, extinguished in the wind, comes not back. I am like the wick of the flame; sorrow unending encircles me like smoke.' She bids him prepare the pyre, so that she may join her husband in death; but a voice from above stays her rash despair and promises her reunion with Kāma, when Śiva's marriage is accomplished. Another way to this end must be found, and in canto V we see Pārvatī seeking to attain the destined aim by devotion to the most terrible austerities, surrounded in the heat of summer by four fires, resting in the rains on bare rocks, spending the nights of winter in icy water. An ascetic comes to her and asks her the purpose of her penance; her sighs reveal that she seeks a lover; her maidens betray her unavowed longing. He warns her of the horrors of her loved one, but she replies:

> In truth thou knowest not Hara, since thus thou dost speak to me. Fools hate the ways of the magnanimous, which are unwonted and unintelligible to them. Auspicious marks are assumed by those who seek to avert misfortune or desire lordship; what has he, on whom the world depends and who is without desire, to do with those whose minds are overcome with desire? Nothing he has, but he is the source of all wealth; he haunts the place of the dead, but he is lord of the three worlds. Dread is his form, yet auspicious is he named; none are there who know the true nature of the bearer of the trident.

[1] This verse is famous through its being borrowed by the prototype of most versions of the *Pañcatantra*.

Śiva, it need hardly be said, cannot resist so glowing an eulogy, and reveals his identity in the seeming ascetic. Canto VI shows us the seven seers, accompanied by Arundhatī, seeking the mountain god, to ask his daughter's hand in marriage; they praise the wooer, while the maiden listens with head downcast as she stands at her father's side, and the father glances to read the decision in his wife's face, 'for as a rule householders follow the lead of their wives in the affairs of their daughters.' The mother indicates assent, and the seers bear back the tidings. The next canto describes the marriage, depicting the mother's mingled joy in the marriage and sorrow at losing her daughter; she cannot paint aright the mark on her child's forehead, or bind correctly her girdle, and the nurse, more sober in her feeling, must remedy her mistakes. In canto VIII Kālidāsa describes with the full detail of the *Kāmaśāstra* the love passages between the newly-wedded pair.

Ānandavardhana[1] assures us that the painting of the love of the deities is in itself apparently a breach of propriety, but that in the hands of the great poet it ceases to offend; but his view evidently did not prevail among ancient critics, and still less, of course, does the conception appeal to Western taste, which finds fault even with the idyllic picture in the *Iliad* of the deceiving of Zeus. But it would be unjust to Kālidāsa to condemn him for a defect in taste, without appreciating the significance of his choice of subject. To Kālidāsa the love of the divine pair is no idle myth; it is reality leading to the birth of a god destined to rescue the world, and the affection of the divine pair is symbolic of the love which ought to be reproduced on earth between husband and wife. Suggestion is the soul of poetry; in the description in the *Kumārasambhava* as in the *Meghadūta* of superhuman love we have the exemplar for love on earth. Viewed thus, the poem gains greatly in attractiveness, and permits us to enjoy the marvellous feeling for nature and power of depicting human emotion which Kālidāsa displays.

Last and greatest of Kālidāsa's Kāvyas is the *Raghuvaṁśa*, the work of his maturity, in which he recounts the glories of the solar race, whose renown doubtless was revived by the

[1] *Dhvanyāloka*, p. 137.

fame of the Guptas, though it is idle to seek any precise parallel between the mythical figures of the past and the historical characters of the early Gupta kings. The solar race is recorded in part in the epic, more largely in the Purāṇas;[1] its mythic character is obvious, and Kālidāsa has eclectically selected for the main theme of his poem a small number of princes, to whom he accords an importance not always given to them in other sources. Dilīpa is the first, pious but childless; Vasiṣṭha tells him the cause of his misfortune; eager to return to his beloved wife from a visit to Indra, he has failed to pay the due meed of homage to Surabhi, Indra's divine cow, and she has cursed him to be without offspring until he win the favour of her daughter. On the sage's advice, he worships by humble imitation the cow Nandinī; a lion leaps on the beast, he offers his own life to save her; the lion reveals himself as a servant of Śiva's, sent to try his courage, and Nandinī, glad at his devotion, grants the boon of a son. Canto III describes the birth and education of the child, young Raghu; entrusted by his father with the guardianship of the sacrificial horse, he fights even with Indra for its possession, and, though he may not conquer the god, yet he wins for his father the fulfilment of his desires. In the next canto is described the glory of Raghu as king and his conquest of the earth; a brilliant picture is unfolded of his triumphant progress; the places he visits, the tribes he subdues, and the battles he wins, are depicted with the most picturesque brevity and force. In canto V we find Raghu reduced to poverty by his generosity; the sage Kautsa pays him a visit to beg alms of him, the king is in a quandary, but his difficulties are solved by a shower of gold which Kubera rains upon his treasure house. His son is Aja, and in canto VI we find him chosen by the princess Indumatī at her Svayaṁvara, the stately ceremonial by which the princesses of the epic are permitted to select for themselves the suitor who most pleases their mind.[2] The princes who come to the meeting are

[1] The view that the extant *Padma Purāṇa* was used by Kālidāsa seems to me disproved by the parallel passages. The Purāṇa may have used Kālidāsa as well as other texts.

[2] J. Przyluski (*Journal Asiatique*, ccv, 101 ff.) finds an Austro-Asiatic origin for this usage.

described with great spirit and brilliance; one is rejected because he is a good gambler, and therefore a bad man; another is excellent, but tastes differ; when the lady of the Court, Sunandā, describes the race of Aja, she sees that he has won her mistress's heart; so, roguishly, she bids her come on to another suitor, but the maiden stays her steps and has her hero crowned with the garland which signifies her choice. In canto VII we learn first of the marriage at which the rejected suitors duly conceal the wrath felt at their defeat, and then of the onslaught made by them on the bridal party as it sets out to the bridegroom's home. Aja shows no trace of fear, but wages war with all his prowess, until, calling to his aid magic weapons given to him by a Gandharva, he causes his foes to sink to sleep, and inscribes on their banners with bloody arrows the boast, 'Raghu's son hath taken from you your fame, but in pity hath left you your lives.' Canto VIII describes with much effect the reign of Aja, which it parallels with the retirement of his sire into the peace of meditation; as the king with his ministers plans the conquest of such lands as remain unsubdued, so the aged father, with learned ascetics, aims at attaining eternal bliss. But a dreadful blow awaits the king; a heavenly garland falls on Indumatī's breast and strikes her dead, and little consolation is it to the prince to be assured that this was no punishment, but that as a nymph of the heaven she had sinned through neglect, and had been forced to earth until she should again see a divine garland. Disconsolate he mourns:

> My constancy is departed; my joy is gone; song is distasteful; spring hath no joy; my jewels are worthless; my couch to-day is left desolate. The mistress of my home, the comrade, the companion of my secret hours, the dear pupil that studied every art with me; in taking thee, say, what of mine hath not pitiless Death reft from me? O fair-eyed one, how canst thou, that hast drunk the nectar of my lips, taste now the offering of water, defiled by my tears, which will reach thee in the other world? For all his possessions what measure of joy can be Aja's without thee? Every joy of mine depended on thee, and nought else could please me.

Impressive, if vain, is the consolation of the sage:

> Enough then of sorrow for her loss; misfortune is the lot of mortals. Be the earth here thy care, for she is the king's true bride. In thy prosperity aforetime thy knowledge of duty was made manifest, in that thou saidst nothing in pride; now again let it be revealed by that

steadfastness, when sorrow has assailed thy heart. Couldst thou by tears win her back? Nay, not even if thou didst follow her in death. The ways of mortals in the world to come depend on their own deeds and are diverse. Lay aside thy sorrow, and honour with due oblation thy spouse: the constant tears of their loved ones burn the dead, so they say. Death is the natural condition for mortals, life a deviation, the wise tell us; if, then, a man but live and breathe for a moment, is not this pure gain to him? It is the fool who deems the loss of a dear one a dart sunk deep in his heart; the wise man knows it a dart removed through the revealing of the way to salvation. The union of the body and the soul and their severance are ordained; say, then, how may the wise man trouble over severance from the world of things? First of the mighty, thou shouldst not, like a common man, fall within the power of sorrow; what difference is there between the tree and the rock, if in the wind both tremble alike?

Nothing availed, however, to heal the sorrow of the king, who welcomed death in his eagerness to rejoin his beloved, and in canto IX we find his son, Daśaratha, reigning. With much brilliance of detail a great hunt is described; there is a fatal ending, for the king by mishap pierces with his arrow the son of an ascetic, and, though in remorse he bears the dying child to his father, the latter in his anger curses the king to die in old age in grief for a son. The end, however, is yet far off; in canto X we learn of the appeal of the gods, threatened by a demon, to Viṣṇu, who condescends himself to become incorporate in the four sons of Daśaratha. In the next canto we are told of Rāma's journey to aid Viśvāmitra against demoniac attacks and his slaughter of Tāḍakā, of his visit to the Court of Janaka of Mithilā, and his winning of Sītā, followed by his victory over Paraśurāma, the exterminator of the Kṣatriya race, who recognises in him the godhead incarnate. Canto XII tells in brief, but with effect, the fatal demand of Kaikeyī for Rāma's banishment and Bharata's coronation, the departure of Rāma and Lakṣmaṇa with Sītā to the forest, their adventures, the rape of Sītā, the efforts of Hanumant to find her, the attack on Laṅkā, and the final victory of Rāma. In canto XIII Kālidāsa lavishes his descriptive power on the account of the return of the united pair in a celestial car, whence they descry the places of their wanderings and sorrows. At the beginning of canto XIV the widows of Daśaratha, who survived only by a little Rāma's departure, receive the visit of their long parted children; Sītā amid the general joy of reunion mourns, with sad foreboding, the sorrow she had brought on her husband. With deliberate art this note of sorrow is followed by the brilliant scene of the royal consecration. But the joy of Ayodhyā is rudely interrupted; evil voices question the purity of the queen, and Rāma, faithful to his conception of duty, must banish her from his side. Sītā, flower of Indian womanhood, endures without reproaches the shame; the seer Vālmīki gives her refuge, and at his hermitage are born her two boys, while Rāma, loving her as ever, dwells in solitude, consoled only by gazing on the golden image which he has had fashioned in her shape. In canto XV Rāma, engaged in the solemn rite of the horse sacrifice, is led to listen to the recitation by two gallant boys of the recital of his deeds, composed by Vālmīki; in wonder he offers the whole earth to the sage, who asks for nothing save the rehabilitation of Sītā, whose children and his the boys are. The king is only too eager to see this accomplished; at an appointed time the sage appears with Sītā and the boys before the people; Sītā drinks holy water, and swears: 'If it be true that I have never in thought, word or deed swerved from my wifely faith, then do thou, O mother earth, take me to thy bosom.' The earth opens, the goddess appears on her snake throne, and takes Sītā in her arms, disappearing into the under-world. Rāma's race is nearly run; the boys, now recognised by all the people as his rightful heirs, are installed in the kingship, and he ascends in solemn state to the sky. The poem has now reached its zenith; canto XVI tells us of a dream which came to Kuśa as he ruled at Kuśāvatī and bade him re-occupy Ayodhyā, his father's capital, while in canto XVII we have the history of the son of Kuśa by a snake princess who was surrendered to him by her father to appease the king's anger at the loss of a bracelet while bathing in the waters which housed the snake king. Cantos XVIII and XIX deal, the first mechanically, with a number of phantom kings from whose names alone the poet derives material for his descriptions, and the latter with the amorous sports of Agnivarman, a worthless libertine whose excesses had the merit of hastening his death. To assert that these cantos are not Kālidāsa's is to go too far,[1] but they certainly do not represent his deliberate

[1] Hillebrandt, *Kālidāsa*, p. 42 f.

workmanship, and we may justly hold that the termination of the poem was prevented by his death.

The more mature genius of Kālidāsa manifests itself in the *Raghuvaṁśa* in his insistence on the Yoga aspect of philosophy rather than on the personal aspect of the divinity in the *Kumārasambhava.* He recognises the three Guṇas or constituents, which make up nature in the Sāṁkhya-Yoga belief and the existence of spirit, but with the Yoga he admits a deity. How precisely he conceived existence, whether the divergences of spirit and matter were for him reconciled in the absolute, we cannot attempt to decide; what is important is that he represents his heroes as seeking release from rebirth by the methods of Yoga, mentioning the technical terms Dhāraṇā, concentration, and Vīrāsana, a special posture deemed suited to aid the attainment of the end desired. He alludes also to the magic powers which Yoga gives, the ability to penetrate a closed door, as well as the higher attainment desired by Sītā of reunion with her beloved in a future life. Viṣṇu, indeed, in the *Raghuvaṁśa* receives his meed of devotion, as was inevitable in an epic of Rāma, but Śiva remains the highest expression of the poet's conception of divinity, for Śiva is a Yogin *par excellence*, though Viṣṇu follows in his train.

We need not seek in Kālidāsa for any solution or suggested solution of the mysteries of life; with the orthodox views of his time he seems to have been fully content; free to choose such episodes of the epic as he pleases, he selects for reproduction the—to modern taste—monstrous denunciation of a Śūdra who has the audacity to practise penance, a privilege which orthodoxy narrowly reserved to the twice-born castes. But in this defect he is in the same case as Sanskrit poets in general, nor would he have admitted that his attitude to life was in any wise lacking. What he would have claimed merit for was his power of evoking by the brilliance of his description the sentiments of love, both as realised in union and as made poignant by separation, of pathos, of heroism, and, last but not least for Indian taste, of the wonderful. He might justly have prided himself on the vividness and precision of his observation and depicting of every side of the world of Indian nature, his skill in bringing before us pictures of the life of India in the Court and the forest, of the princely Svayaṁvara, of the marriage rite, of the battle, and his achievement in reducing to effective brevity the famous but lengthy epic tale of the *Rāmāyaṇa*. In the description of Raghu's conquests we need not seek for parallelism in detail with the achievements of Samudragupta and Chandragupta, but we have in it the poetic reflex of the achievements of these great Emperors; as ever Kālidāsa effects his aim not by direct means but by suggestion; just as Virgil glorifies Rome and incidentally the imperial dynasty by his *Æneid*, so Kālidāsa extols the sway of the Guptas and the Brahmanical restoration by reminding his audience of the glories of the far gone days of the solar race.

The Kāvya style unquestionably attains in Kālidāsa its highest pitch, for in him the sentiment predominates over the ornaments, which serve to enhance it, instead of overwhelming it. Sentiment with him is the soul of poetry, and, fond as he is of the beauty due to the use of figures, he refrains from sacrificing his main purpose in the search for effect. Indian poetics, we must admit, often mistook the trees for the wood, and by the enormous development of sub-divisions of figures (*alaṁkāras*) conveyed the impression that to write poetry one must be ever striving to introduce figures of one sort or another. Kālidāsa himself, in canto IX of the *Raghuvaṁśa*, has chosen to show to us his skill in poetical artifice. He here not merely uses a remarkable number of metres, fourteen in all, of which thirteen occur in the verses 55–82, but he displays his skill in Yamakas, paronomasias, the repetition of the same syllable in various forms with change of meaning. This artifice is pleasing to modern taste chiefly when the sound is skilfully wedded, as not rarely in Kālidāsa, to the sense; thus the verse, *raṇareṇavo rurudhire rudhireṇa suradviṣām*, 'the dust of the field of battle grew stiff with the blood of the foes of the gods,' is redeemed from triviality by the matching of sound and sense. Great stress, however, is laid by Indian poetics on the subject of sound (*śabda*); Kālidāsa is approved for using such a Yamaka as *bhujalatām* and *jaḍatām* because *l* and *ḍ*, like *l* and *r*, and *v* and *b*, are permitted as analogous in Yamakas. An essential feature of the Vaidarbha style which is attributed to him is the use of pleasing sounds, so that the employment of harsh combinations as in *ṛddhyai* and *labdhyai*, is censured by Mammaṭa. In canto XVIII of the *Raghuvaṁśa* we find alliteration practised with special frequency, and, as in canto IX, we can see no reason for the adoption of what appeals to us rather as an affectation. Much more interesting to modern taste are figures of thought (*arthālaṁkāra*), a term which, as distinguished from Śabdālaṁkāra, does not correspond to the Western distinction of figures of thought and of speech, but comprehends all figures which are not merely concerned with sound. In the use of such figures Kālidāsa is particularly happy, and is cited repeatedly as a model by the writers on poetics. His *forte* is declared to lie in similes, and the praise is well deserved. True, the world of India is a different one from the West; the divine mythology and the belief of everyday life are far other, but even so the beauty and force of many of the similes and metaphors must be recognised by anyone who appreciates poetry. With glad eyes the maidens of the city follow the king, as the nights with the clear stars of autumn the pole star. The weapons of the foe so beset the chariot of the prince that it may be recognised by the tip of its banner alone, as the pale sun alone reveals the morning enveloped in the mist. Dilīpa hears in the leaves his fame sung by the goddesses of the wood to the sound of the reed, which whistles in the wind and plays the part of the flute. The wound torn by the arrow is the gate of death, the stone hurled at the foe the torn-off hand of the god of death; the battlefield is a banquet for that grim god. Characteristic is the carrying out of the simile in precise detail, in striking contrast to the Homeric manner where the detail is given as a picture but parallelism is not sought. The mountain is a wild bull, its caves are its mouth, its peaks are its horns, the clouds the earth which it tears up in play, and its thundering cataracts its wild bellowing.

More natural than this to modern feeling is the constant attribution of life to things inanimate; joy, sorrow, and every feeling of man can be attributed to the mountains and the streams; Rāvaṇa's fall frees the sun from tribulation; the winds respectfully greet the royal pair. Less appeal is made to us by similes from the fields of philosophy or grammar; the king sets forth to overcome the Persians, as the ascetic conquers the senses by the knowledge of reality; Sugrīva is installed king in his brother's place, as a substitute is used for the normal root. Politics also yields its store; the mountains, which Indra deprives of their wings, flee to the sea, as princes in misfortune to a neutral lord. Often the same subject is illustrated by a series of similes carefully elaborated in detail; the mixture of ideas is conspicuously lacking. In the drama we find humorous similes, but humour is hardly to be found in the epics or lyrics.

Of the other figures Kālidāsa makes free and happy use; especially marked is his skill in the Arthāntaranyāsa, which consists in expressing in a general proposition an idea exhibited in particular form in the preceding three lines of a stanza; the continuation of the *Kumārasambhava* shows clearly its unauthenticity by the feebleness of its efforts at this figure. It is important to note that he shows little fondness for the use of the Śleṣa[1] or double entendre, a fact which tells incidentally against the view that Dignāga is referred to in this manner in v. 14 of the *Meghadūta.*

[1] E.g. *Raghuvaṁśa*, xi, 20; *Kumārasambhava*, viii, 22.

IV

POST-KĀLIDĀSAN EPIC

WE have seen in Kālidāsa the style which the text-books on poetics from the *Kāvyādarsa* downwards style Vaidarbhan, and in a poem of much pretension, but small merit, written in A.D. 472–73 by Vatsabhaṭṭi, a Praśasti, or panegyric, of the temple of the sun at Mandasor, we have a specimen of poetry which illustrates the style of the Gauḍas as described by Daṇḍin, the manner of Eastern as opposed to Southern or Western poets. The poem is of interest in that the correct title is omitted, being indicated only by the gender of the adjective alluding to it at the close of the poem; Praśastis were evidently so common that the noun was easily supplied by the reader. Further the poet claims to have composed with effort (*prayatnena*); in fact, he makes every attempt to show his knowledge of the rules of the Kāvya; he finds room for an allusion to the land of Lāṭa, describes at length the city Daśapura, and includes in his 44 stanzas descriptions of both the spring and the winter. He uses no less than twelve metres, especially the Vasantatilaka, and he carries on the sense often over two, three or more stanzas, all in the best Kāvya style. Conclusive for his appertaining to the Eastern school is his use of long compounds in verse, even to the extent of filling a whole half-stanza, more often to filling a line. This is precisely one point in which an essential distinction between the Vaidarbha and the Gauḍa styles exists. Secondly, in v. 26 he carefully assimilates the sound to the sentiment to be conveyed, changing the smooth and pleasant sound of the first three lines, which describe the goodness and wisdom of the king, to harsh syllables in the last line, where his dread power is alluded to, 'alone skilled to destroy the haughty hosts of the foe (*dviṭdṛpta-*

pakṣakṣapaṇaikadakṣaḥ).' On the other hand, there are clear traces of the imitation of both the *Meghadūta* and the *Ṛtusaṁhāra*.[1]

It would be interesting to know when the divergence of Eastern and Southern styles was first recognised, but the evidence available is inadequate to permit of any determination. It has been suggested[2] that the tendency to the simpler style of the South was given, in opposition to the affectation and bombast, the love of alliteration, and the use of recondite phraseology of the East, by the influence of the poetry of Mahārāṣṭra, which probably came into being after the beginning of the third century A.D. and is first known to us from the anthology of Hāla, who may perhaps be identified with the Sātavāhana of Pratiṣṭhāna, to whom the Jain tradition attributes in A.D. 467 the reformation of the Calendar of the Church. The conjecture, however, lacks any secure foundation; it is more likely that the style of the Māhāraṣṭrī lyric was influenced by the pre-existing Vaidarbha style, and it is noteworthy that in the *Nāṭyaśāstra* we have already the merits of the style which in Daṇḍin is given that name asserted generally as those of the Kāvya. The Eastern style, then, may be treated not so much as an old and decadent one, but as a further development, and this accords with the fact that, in practice as opposed to the theory of the writers on poetics, it is the Gauḍa style which prevails in later Sanskrit epics.

The history of the epic, in fact, is one of decline in taste and growing artificiality of form. The earlier epics, however, are not without merit. Tradition would make contemporaneous with Kālidāsa the *Setubandha*,[3] a poem in Māhārāṣṭrī, which elicits praise from Daṇḍin and Bāṇa, but the long compounds and artificial style disprove this. Before Bāṇa

[1] Bühler, *Die indischen Inschriften*, pp. 8 ff.; Kielhorn, *Gött. Nach.*, 1890, pp. 251 ff.; *Ind. Ant.*, xix, 285. Hoernle's objections (*J.R.A.S.*, 1909, p. 111) are ineffective.

[2] H. Jacobi, *Ausgewählte Erzählungen in Māhārāṣṭrī*, pp. xv ff. Bāṇa notes the Western love of sense, not sound, and the Southern play of fancy. Historically it seems probable that Sanskrit poetry flourished comparatively late in the East; cf. S. K. Chatterji, *Bengali Language*, i, 73 ff.; H. Chakladar, *A.B.I.*, viii, 46 ff.

[3] Ed. and trs. S. Goldschmidt, 1880–84; ed. *Kāvyamālā*, No. 47, 1895.

also we may place the date of Bhāravi, since in the Aihole inscription of A.D. 634 he already appears as famous, but presumably the period was not great enough to allow his reputation to elicit from Bāṇa the meed of praise one would expect. Certainly later than Kālidāsa, Bhāravi displays gifts of no mean order. The subject of his *Kirātārjunīya*[1] is derived from the Vanaparvan of the *Mahābhārata*,[2] which tells us how the sage, Vyāsa, advised the Pāṇḍavas to leave the Dvaita forest, and when they had done so Yudhiṣṭhira urges Arjuna to obtain celestial weapons for the fight with the Kauravas to gain the kingdom. Arjuna obeys, proceeds to the Himālayas, meeting *en route* an ascetic who seeks to turn him from his purpose of practising penance to win divine favour, but, when he fails to dissuade him, reveals himself and gives him his blessing. Attaining his goal, Arjuna practises penance, and after a conflict with Śiva under the guise of a Kirāta obtains from his conqueror the weapons he desires. In Bhāravi's hands the epic tale is not unsuccessfully embellished. A new motif is introduced in canto I; a spy, sent by Yudhiṣṭhira to report on the state of his foe, Suyodhana, brings back the evil news of the virtue of his rule, which wins the heart of the people; Draupadī, then, as in the epic, urges immediate war. Bhīma adds his voice to hers, but Yudhiṣṭhira hesitates thus to break the compact he had made (II). Vyāsa appears, and bids Arjuna in preparation for war attain the aid of Indra; a Yakṣa is sent by him to be Arjuna's companion in his quest (III). The journey to the Himālaya affords opportunity for a fine description of the autumn and of the life of the herdsmen (IV), and the mountain itself is vividly depicted at length (V). The penance of Arjuna begins; its austerity causes panic to the Guhyakas, spirits of the mountain, who bear the news to Indra; he shares their fears and bids the Apsarases and the Gandharvas break in on his penance (VI). The divine hosts fly to the place of the hero's abode; the elephants of the divine host are described at length (VII), as are the plucking of flowers by the maidens and their bathing in the Ganges (VIII). The poet then describes the approach of evening, the rise of

[1] Ed. Bombay, 1907; *Trivandrum Sanskrit Series*, No. 63, 1918.
[2] iii, 27–41.

the moon, the love play, and the dawn of day (IX). Then the Apsarases turn all the forces of their charms on Arjuna, only to be foiled by his superb constancy (X). Indra himself undertakes the task; he appears in disguise, praises his efforts, but comments on the contrast between his acts and his martial equipment; Arjuna perseveres in his purpose, and is rewarded by the god's approval, and the advice to win Śiva's favour (XI). The poet has thus embellished out of recognition the simplicity of the epic, with the disadvantage that in canto XII we have again the motif of his extreme asceticism, followed by the report of the perturbed Ṛṣis to Śiva. The master explains the purpose of the hero, whom the demon Mūka in boar shape purposes to slay, and with his host hastens to the spot. Arjuna and Śiva alike let fly their arrows at the boar, but, as Arjuna claims it as his prey, he is confronted by a Kirāta who asserts his right (XII–XIII). A struggle follows; the host of Śiva shatters itself in vain on the hero; it is re-formed by Skanda and Śiva himself, and a terrible battle ensues between the god and the warrior, in which both use miraculous weapons, until the god reveals himself to Arjuna, receiving from him a hymn of praise and supplication, which he rewards with the grant of magic arms. The employment of Śiva's host and of the supernatural weapons on either side are innovations.

It would be unjust to deny both poetical fancy and force of diction to Bhāravi; the sentiment of heroism is admirably expressed, and the descriptions of scenery are often brilliant. But the artificiality of his work is also often painful; his use of figures is unceasing and fatiguing in its complex variety, and in canto XV he descends to trivialities in the worst Alexandrian type; he produces stanzas which give the same sounds and sense read forwards and backwards, or present the same line to be read in four different senses, or contain syllables beginning with *c* and *r* only, or exhibit no consonant save *n*, except a solitary final *t*. One stanza gives a threefold sense, and in all we have tortured language. Similarly the poet is accomplished in grammar; he obeys minute rules of Pāṇini and achieves the rare distinction of confining the imperfect to the purpose of describing the experiences of the user in matters not of the same day, while the aorist deals with events of the same day, leaving the perfect for matters experienced by others.[1] The accuracy of use is purely a learned pedantry; Aśvaghoṣa and Kālidāsa earlier, and Māgha later, have nothing of the kind.

A logical carrying out to the utmost of the same pedantry is seen in the *Bhaṭṭi-kāvya*, whose author describes in 22 cantos the tale of the *Rāmāyaṇa* for the purpose of illustrating the niceties of Sanskrit grammar. It is true that the work is not without passages of poetic merit, but they are far too few to give it any serious literary value, though it has the interest of affording an exposition of the practical effect of the rules of the grammar as understood by the author, who is also of value for his contributions to our knowledge of the rhetorical figures which he often in canto X illustrates. His date is uncertain; the author, indeed, lets us know that he wrote at Valabhī under Śrīdharasena, but the identification of that king is, owing to the similarity of the names of the recorded rulers, not beyond dispute; perhaps most probable is the middle of the seventh century A.D. The name more than anything else has suggested identification with the famous Bhartṛhari, but without plausibility.[2]

Yet another Rāma epic is the *Jānakīharaṇa* of Kumāradāsa, which the poet Rājaśekhara (A.D. 900) mentions in comparison with the *Raghuvaṁśa*, high praise but not altogether undeserved. Fourteen cantos with a part of the fifteenth, all that is left of the original 25, have been restored from a Sinhalese word-for-word version, bringing the story down to Aṅgada's mission to bid Rāvaṇa render up Sītā. As usual, the author's chief aim is description; thus in canto I Ayodhyā, the king, and his wives receive their meed of honour; in III the sport of the sovereign in the water with his wives, sunset, night and morning; in VII Sītā, in VIII the love play of the married pair, as in *Kumārasambhava* VIII, with a fine description of sunset and night; in XIV the causeway built by the apes over the ocean; spring (II), the rainy season (XI) and autumn (XII) are also duly depicted; Kumāradāsa's style is less simple than that of Kālidāsa, and he is extremely fond of alliterations, which give his verses a singularly easy flow, thus

[1] Cappeller's trans., pp. 176 ff.

[2] H. Jacobi, *Sitzungsber. d. Preussischen Akademie*, 1922, p. 216 f. Ed. *Bombay Sanskrit Series*, 1898, Nos. 56 and 57.

attaining the softness and mellifluousness of the Vaidarbha style. His love of periphrases is noteworthy, and he is skilled in depicting both the pretty and the grandiose. His date is dubious; that he was a king of Ceylon (A.D. 517–26) seems no more than a fable; he appears to know the *Kāśikā Vṛtti*, which dates from about A.D. 650, and possibly he belongs to the latter part of that century.[1]

It is probable, rather than certain, that both the *Bhaṭṭikāvya* and the *Jānakīharaṇa* were known to Māgha, who certainly used freely both Kālidāsa and Bhāravi and who may be assigned, on the strength of the evidence of an inscription referring to a relative, to about A.D. 700, though this date is certainly not without difficulty of its own. His grandfather was Suprabhadeva, minister of the king Varmalāta, and his father Dattaka Sarvāśraya. It is clear that he knew the *Nāgānanda*, to which a reference is made in his Kāvya (XX, 44); the effort to prove that he was used by Subandhu may be regarded as definitely disproved.[2]

The *Śiśupālavadha* in 20 cantos is based on an episode in the *Mahābhārata*. Yudhiṣṭhira, after the conquest of Jarāsandha of Magadha, is the first ruler in India, and has performed the solemn sacrifice of the Rājasūya, or royal consecration. At the close, gifts of honour are to be distributed; the wise Bhīṣma allots to Kṛṣṇa the first, but against this Śiśupāla, king of Cedi, raises bitter protest; hence flows a quarrel which ends only with the slaying of Śiśupāla by Kṛṣṇa, who earlier had won his enmity by enticing away the bride destined for him. The theme is obviously inadequate to support an epic, but the defect is made good by the usual luxuriance of erotic and other descriptions in which Māgha endeavours, every now and then with brilliant success, to improve on the ideas expressed in the stanzas of his predecessors. His chief merit lies

[1] F. W. Thomas, *J.R.A.S.*, 1901, pp. 253 ff.; Keith, pp. 578 ff.; i–x ed. and trs. Nandargikar, Bombay, 1907, who places the author later. The London School of Oriental Studies has a text in twenty cantos, of which xvi is printed in its *Bulletin*, iv, 285 ff.

[2] Kielhorn, *Gött. Nach.*, 1906, pp. 143 ff. Cf. Jacobi, *Vienna Or. Journ.*, iii, 121 ff.; D. R. Bhandarkar, *Ep. Ind.*, ix, 187 ff.; E. Hultzsch, trans., (Leipzig, 1926), pp. iv–vii, who (p. 219, n. 3) denies the allusion to the *Nāgānanda*, but without cogent grounds.

precisely in some of these word pictures, whose merits need not be denied, despite the effort requisite to extricate them from tedious conceits. His experiments in reviving rare grammatical usages have already been referred to, and he successfully vies with Bhāravi in the effort to produce absurdities; thus XIX, 34, read backwards is identical with the preceding stanza read in the ordinary way, and many other stanzas in that canto are equally devoid of anything save the most tasteless grotesqueness; for instance, the power to form a sword or lotus or wheel shape. Māgha's reputation later doubtless rests in some degree on the vitiation of taste which, as in the Alexandrian age of Greek poetry, admitted his strained effects, but he had undoubtedly no mean talent. His metrical profusion is wonderful; Bhāravi uses but twenty-four metres, while he has forty-one, and, though many are merely sporadic, whole series of verses occur in rare metres, such as the Udgatā in XV, Mañjubhāṣiṇī in XIII, Rucirā in XIII and Svāgatā in X.[1] His vocabulary is copious and his command of the ornaments of style profound.

In the early part of the eighth century falls the Prākrit poem, *Gaüḍavaha*[2] of Vākpati, which is but a selection of series of connected verses, extracted from the prelude to what would have been a vast account of the overthrow of a Gauḍa prince by his patron Yaśovarman of Kanauj, had not a just fate spared us the completion of the work through the downfall of the poet's patron before Lalitāditya of Kashmir about A.D. 736. The poet admits indebtedness to Bhavabhūti, and his work is chiefly of interest because in the size of its compounds it is a perfect masterpiece of bad style. Full of conventional descriptions, and extremely vague as we have it, it has no claim to be ranked even as embryo history, but it shows how closely Prākrit poetry kept pace with Sanskrit poetry in the degradation of style.

The ultimate result of the love of playing with language which marks both Bhāravi and Māgha is seen in the *Rāghava-pāṇḍavīya* of Kavirāja, which is most probably to be dated under the Kādamba Kāmadeva about A.D. 1190, though it

[1] Kālidāsa has 6 main and 13 subordinate metres; Bhāravi 12 and 12; Māgha 17 and 24.

[2] Cf. H. Jacobi, *Gött gel. Anz.*, 1888, pp. 61 ff.; ed. *Bombay Sanskrit Series*, No. 34.

has been ascribed to the ninth century.[1] It aims at telling the tale of Rāma and of the *Mahābhārata* simultaneously, a result which is only possible because of the large number of meanings which are assigned to Sanskrit words by the lexicons, the diverse modes in which members of compounds may be connected, and the different ways in which the syllables composing a line can be conjoined. It is fair to say that, considering the appalling nature of the task undertaken, the poet, whose name is lost to the obloquy he merits, shows very considerable skill, and might have produced a meritorious work had he devoted his efforts to a more legitimate end. Equally negligible as literature is the *Kavirahasya*[2] of Halāyudha, written in the tenth century to illustrate in the manner of the *Bhaṭṭikāvya* the rules of verbal formation.

Equal lack of taste is shown in the enormous size of the *Haravijaya*[3] of the Kashmirian poet, Rājānaka Ratnākara Vāgīśvara, who flourished under the kings Bṛhaspati, or Cippaṭa Jayāpīḍa, and Avantivarman, and thus must have been in his prime about A.D. 850. The fifty cantos in four thousand long stanzas deal with a tiny plot, the slaying of Andhaka by Śiva. This demon sprung from Śiva himself, when Pārvatī playfully covered his eyes with her hands, and was born blind. He was given to a son of Diti who reared him, and in due course by appalling austerities he regained sight, made war on the gods, and became master of the three worlds, until Śiva slew him. The scanty matter is eked out by the inevitable descriptions; thus Śiva's capital must be described (I), his Tāṇḍava dance (II), the seasons (III), mount Mandara (IV–V); a little action now intervenes; the seasons, Spring at their head, flee to Śiva for aid against the conqueror of heaven (VI); the consultations of Śiva's hosts as to the action to be taken cover up to canto XVI, giving an admirable opportunity for a display of the poet's erudition in the science of politics. An envoy is finally sent to bid the

[1] Ed. *Kāvyamālā*, No. 62, 1897. Cf. Keith, *Bodl. Catal. App.*, p. 27; Pischel, *Die Hofdichter des Lakṣmaṇasena*, p. 37. A work of the same title by Dhanaṁjaya is mentioned by a Rājaśekhara, and the date of it is dubious. Cf. Fleet, *Ind. Ant.*, xxxiii, 279.

[2] Ed. L. Heller, Greifswald, 1900.

[3] Ed. *Kāvyamālā*, No. 22, 1890. For his rare words see *Vienna Oriental Journal*, xxix, 259 ff.

demon abandon the throne he has usurped. As an interlude now follow thirteen cantos devoted to the sports of Śiva's attendants, including the usual amusements of the harem, the gathering of flowers and amorous play, the sunrise, the setting of the sun, the stormy sea. In canto XXX the ambassador arrives, and for seven cantos after XXXI, which must, of course, describe heaven at length, we have challenge and defiance. The return of the envoy and the preparations of Śiva for battle occupy the next four cantos (XXXIX–XLII), while the battle fills the rest, with an interlude of a hymn in praise of the goddess Caṇḍī (XLVII). The poem is animated by a desire to vie with Bāṇa in style; it has all the involutions and contortions of Māgha, and is full of Yamakas, involving as always a sacrifice of sense to sound. Amid these defects the merits of single lines or passages can be realised with difficulty.

Kashmir produced also in the eleventh century the multitudinous works of Kṣemendra, which includes summaries of the epics, the *Bhāratamañjarī* and the *Rāmāyaṇamañjarī*, which are poetically worthless. A century later, however, about A.D. 1135–45, we have the *Śrīkaṇṭhacarita*[1] of Maṅkha, which in twenty-five cantos describes the destruction of the demon Tripura, by Śiva. The topic is merely the excuse for various exercises in poetical skill; thus benedictions and prayers occupy canto I; descriptions of the good and bad, etc., in II and III are followed by an account of Kailāsa (IV), its lord (V), the spring (VI), the game of swinging (VII), the plucking of flowers (VIII), sporting in the water (IX), the dusk (X), the moon (XI), the rising of the moon (XII), and so on until in XVIII–XXI we have the account of the trouble among, and the preparations for battle of, Śiva's hosts. The battle (XXIII) and the burning of the city of Tripura (XXIV) are preceded by an account of the panic of the Daityas (XXII). Finally, by a happy change in canto XXV, we have an account of the persons making up the Sabhā or darbar of the poet's brother Alaṁkāra, a minister of Jayasiṁha (A.D. 1129–50). Apart from its value for history the canto is interesting in its painting of the procedure of such a darbar, one of the chief modes of social intercourse among the learned of India. Otherwise the epic must be confessed to be dreary and uninteresting.

[1] Ed. *Kāvyamālā*, No. 3, 1887.

The same verdict may be passed still more emphatically on the *Naiṣadhīya*[1] of Śrī-Harṣa, the logician, perhaps of Bengal, author of the *Khaṇḍanakhaṇḍakhādya*, in which he defends the Vedānta by the desperate means of showing that all views on philosophical topics are indefensible. His date is the latter part of the twelfth century A.D. under Jayaccandra of Kanauj. His *Naiṣadhīya* ranks with Kālidāsa's epics, and those of Bhaṭṭi, Bhāravi and Māgha as a Mahākāvya *par excellence*. It would hardly have occurred to anyone with a modicum of good taste to disfigure, as he has done, the simple beauty of the story of Nala and Damayantī, as it is presented in the epic, by turning a short part of it into the theme of twenty-two cantos in the most elaborate Kāvya style, abounding in alliterations of the Yamaka type. The frank and attractive love picture of the epic is overwhelmed with all the most pedantic developments of the *Kāmaśāstra*. No fewer than nineteen metres are employed, and any trace of poetic thought is hard or impossible to find. The same condemnation applies to the *Nalodaya*, of late but uncertain date, perhaps written by a poet of Kerala, Vāsudeva, possibly in the fourteenth century, which in four cantos deals with Nala's story from the point of view of his restoration to fortune. As often in late texts, it frequently shows both end and middle rimes, and canto II is the usual attempt to turn the *Kāmaśāstra* into poetry.

The tendency to introduce rime in Sanskrit poems is doubtless of popular origin, as is shown by the fact that Apabhraṁśa poetry is full of rime. In Sanskrit poetry we have, elaborated by both Daṇḍin and Vāmana among the writers on poetics, the use of Yamakas, groups of identical syllables recurring in the stanza especially at the end of the lines. The Yamaka gives a true rime only when the vowel of the first syllable of the group is preceded by a different consonant, and when the syllables which thus nearly agree are found in the corresponding parts of lines; the normal end rime is first defined in the *Sāhityadarpaṇa* of works on theory, although it is known to Hemacandra in his *Chandonuśāsana*, though not mentioned in his poetics. In the former

[1] Ed. Bombay, 1894. Cf. Nilkamal Bhattacharya, *Sarasvati Bhavana Studies*, iii, 159 ff.

text it is styled end alliteration (*antyānuprāsa*), and Hemacandra applies to it the term alliteration in opposition to Yamaka. Yamakas are not rare in Prākrit, being common in the *Setubandha*. On the other hand, deliberate, as opposed to occasional, riming is late in Sanskrit poetry, and even in Prākrit it cannot be said to be regular or frequent.[1]

In addition to those mentioned, many other epics are known by name or exist in manuscript. One from whose author the anthologies have preserved some graceful verses is the *Kapphaṇābhyudaya* of Śivasvāmin, who was a Court poet of the well-known Avantivarman of Kashmir, and therefore flourished before the end of the ninth century. The author was a Buddhist, and, therefore chooses a legend known from the *Avadānaśataka*, where we learn of a king of the Dakṣiṇāpatha who menaces the lord of Śrāvastī, but is converted and becomes an Arhant. This theme is embellished in twenty cantos in the manner of Māgha. We have the description of the capital Līlāvatī, and the king (I); the account brought to him by a spy of Prasenajit's just rule and pride, which the spy urges the monarch to bend. Then follow the agitation of the kings of the Court at the news (III), the council of war (IV), and the mission of an envoy to bear the threat of war to Prasenajit (V). The king then, on the advice of a Vidyādhara, visits the Malaya mountain to devise with him a plan of campaign (VI). The opportunity is thus afforded to describe the encampment of the host (VII), the seasons which all unite on the mountain (VIII), the amusement of picking flowers (X), preceded by sports in the water (IX), the sunset (XI), the rising of the moon (XII), drinking (XIII), the delights of love (XIV), followed by the end of the night and daybreak (XV). The march (XVI) and the battle (XVII-XIX) lead up to the *finale*, the conversion of Kapphaṇa. Throughout the tricks of Māgha's style are imitated, and the author also clearly follows the *Nāgānanda* when he describes the heaps of bones of Nāgas slain by Garuḍa heaped on the seashore beyond the Malaya mountain.[2]

[1] H. Jacobi, *Bhavisattakaha*, pp. 51 ff.

[2] Śeshagiri Śāstri, *Reports*, ii, 49 ff. The king's name appears also as Kappaṇa. It is known to Bhoja's *Śṛṅgāraprakāśa*.

V

HISTORICAL KĀVYA

AMONG the Kāvyas so far mentioned there is none that can be called historical, but the material for history is presented by the Kāvya inscriptions, which normally refer to some definite event, and sometimes give genealogical details of alleged descent. Kālidāsa, as we have seen, prefers to hint at the greatness of the Guptas in the *Raghuvaṁśa* rather than describe their deeds as sober history, and it may be true, as the legend insists, that the *Setubandha*[1] was written indirectly to celebrate the building of a bridge of boats across the Vitastā by king Pravarasena of Kashmir. That this should be the earliest form of historical composition is natural enough; there were obvious rewards awaiting the poet who could either directly or indirectly—as perhaps in the title of the *Kumārasambhava* if it allude to Kumāragupta's birth—gratify a patron; to compose history for its own sake was a conception which in any land is slow to emerge, and in India in particular came very late and imperfectly into being. The explanation of this omission is doubtless too complex to permit of precise evaluation.[2] Certainly much must be accounted for by the conception of life held by the Brahmins; the belief in the constant evolution and involution of the world, in endless periods of recurrence, in the power of transmigration, and the acceptance of the intermingling of divine and human action in the world must have served to

[1] This may be thought to favour the view that the poem was Kālidāsa's, written for Pravarasena; H. Jacobi, *Bhavisattakaha*, p. 83, n. 1. Contrast Peterson, *Kādambarī*, p. 77. Another claimant is the Vākāṭaka Pravarasena II. No result is possible on the existing evidence. Cf. S. K. Aiyangar, *A.B.I.*, v, 44 f.; Peterson, *J.R.A.S.*, 1926, p. 725 f.

[2] H. Oldenberg, *Aus dem Alten Indien*, pp. 65 ff.

blunt the value placed upon, and the appreciation of, the importance of history. The same spirit tended against the creation of any history; the dynasties might war against one another, there might be convulsions in the royal houses themselves, but no great change came over the life of the people; the handbooks of policy show no consciousness of political evolution, but deal merely with the preservation and extension of kingdoms, based on factors which are regarded as invariable. In the history even of thought India was uninterested; the works which deal with philosophical systems give us no information regarding the chronological interrelations of the schools, and are content to accept any anachronism. If this is true of the Brahmin intellectual aristocracy, we need not be surprised that the Kṣatriyas asked no more than panegyrics of their own deeds and genealogies, flattering if manifestly untrue. From another point of view the ancient heroes of the epic seemed as real to the Indians as the historical rulers of the day, and more so than their predecessors in the past; it was, therefore, infinitely more interesting to preserve such a poem as the *Naiṣadhīya*, dealing with persons famous throughout India, than a mere historical account of local kings, whose fame scarcely extended beyond the circumscribed limits of their own domains.

It is not, therefore, surprising that the first historic Kāvya preserved to us is deliberately built on the romantic model. The *Harṣacarita*[1] of Bāṇa belongs to the middle of the seventh century A.D.; as it is unfinished, we may assume that the author was carried off by death before he could complete his purpose. Yet it seems as if he commenced it at least before he wrote the *Kādambarī*, which likewise he left incomplete. The work passes in the theory as the model of an Ākhyāyikā; it begins with an elaborate account of the quite mythical origin of the poet's race, which fills a whole chapter, styled Ucchvāsa. Further details are given of the writer's personal history (II); his mother, Rājyadevī, died when he was a child, so that his father filled for him the part of both parents. He also died when Bāṇa was fourteen; the child felt his loss deeply, but in the course of time his spirits revived. We are told of his

[1] Ed. P. V. Kane, Bombay, 1918; S. D. and A. B. Gajendragadkar, Poona, 1919.

pursuits and his comrades, leading up to a narrative of an invitation received from Harṣadeva to visit his Court. On his return thence he was asked to undertake a description of the deeds of the king and consented to tell a part, though the whole were an impossible burden (III). We are then given the tale of Harṣa, beginning in effect with his father, Prabhākaravardhana, the death of that monarch, the murder of his eldest son, Rājyavardhana, Harṣavardhana's successful effort to save his sister, Rājyaśrī, and his return with her. The total sum of his story recounted is thus no more than an incident, and even it cannot be said to be presented in any satisfactory fashion; intentionally, or otherwise, Bāṇa leaves many points in his narrative obscure, especially the position and actions of the Mālava and Gauḍa kings, who slew respectively Grahavarman, husband of Harṣa's sister, Rājyaśrī, and his brother. There may have been excellent reasons for glossing over the events, but at any rate the picture is blurred and uncertain. On the other hand, the whole resources of Bāṇa's romantic style are applied to embellish the theme; as in the *Kādambarī*, he aims at vying with Subandhu's power of illustration and description, and in Ucchvāsa VIII alone two-fifths of the text are taken up by five long descriptions. The style is often simply irritating; there is no true pathos in a description[1] which represents the unhappy Rājyaśrī as

> with her kindred and her graces all gone, her ears and her soul left bare, her ornaments and her aims abandoned, her bracelets and her hopes broken, her companions and the needle-like grass spears clinging round her feet, her eye and her beloved fixed within her bosom, her sight and her hair long, her limbs and her merits exhausted, her aged attendants and her streaming tears falling down at her feet.

On the other hand, Bāṇa at his best is master of forceful description,[2] as in the account of Harṣa's march out or of the last moments of Prabhākaravardhana:

> He was on the confines of doom, on the verge of the last gasp, at the outset of the great undertaking, at the portal of the long sleep, on the tip of death's tongue, broken in utterance, unhinged in mind, tortured in body, waning in life, babbling in speech, ceaseless in sighs, vanquished by yawning, swayed by suffering, in the bondage of racking pains.

[1] Cowell and Thomas's version (London, 1897).
[2] For other cases, see the trans., pp. 201, 205.

The preface to the work is of special importance, since it mentions as famous the author of the *Vāsavadattā*, Bhaṭṭāra Haricandra, Sātavāhana, Pravarasena, Bhāsa, Kālidāsa, and the author of the *Bṛhatkathā*, thus giving us some valuable information on literary history.

Later historical works prefer the poetic form pure and simple. One of the earliest of importance is the *Navasāhasāṅkacarita*[1] of Padmagupta or Parimala, son of Mṛgāṅkagupta, who was a protégé of the kings of Dhārā, first of Vākpatirāja, then of his successor, Sindhurāja, at whose direction his Kāvya was written. Like all works intended as panegyrics, its value for historical purposes cannot be placed high, nor is it distinguished as a Kāvya. More interesting is the *Vikramāṅkadevacarita*[2] of Bilhaṇa, written to celebrate the reign of the Cālukya Vikramāditya VI of Kalyāṇa. Bilhaṇa, author of the play *Karṇasundarī*[3] and the *Caurapañcāśikā*, was born in Kashmir, where his father, Jyeṣṭhakalaśa, was a grammarian; he studied the Vedas, grammar, and poetics there, and left his native land about A.D. 1065, after the nominal accession of Kalaśa to the throne, to win fame and fortune in India, fate eventually securing him the post of Court poet at Kalyāṇa, where he wrote his epic probably about A.D. 1085. The poem exhibits, taken as historic, similar defects to the work of Bāṇa; it gives a sketchy and imperfect account of the predecessors of its hero, glosses over the struggles which brought him to the throne in lieu of his elder brother, and introduces Śiva thrice to explain the embarrassing fact that the king evidently achieved the throne by conduct the reverse of fraternal. We are assured of his defeats and annihilation of the Colas, but the exaggeration of these assertions is proved by the fact that these ubiquitous enemies immediately after are revealed as attacking once more. We learn later (XIV–XV) of a war against another brother, Jayasiṁha, and in canto XVII the Colas again require to be suppressed, but throughout there is a haughty disdain of chronological accuracy, which renders the work inferior even to a mediæval

[1] Ed. *Bombay Sanskrit Series*, No. 53.

[2] Ed. *Bombay Sanskrit Series*, No. 14.

[3] See Konow, *Das indische Drama*, p. 113; Keith, *Sanskrit Drama*, p. 256.

chronicle as a source of precise information. The extent of the work is made up to seventeen cantos by wholesale exploitation of Kāvya topics. Thus cantos VII–XIII are engrossed with the tale of the winning of his queen, Candralekhā, daughter of a Śilahāra prince of Karahāta; in VII the effect of spring in arousing the passion of love and the amusements of the season are depicted; in VIII the loveliness of the princess is described; then follows the account of her Svayaṁvara, at which, disdaining the other princes, she chooses the Cālukyan as her spouse, while the other suitors cherish feelings of hate. An account follows of the sports of the pair, both in the game of the swing and in the water, of the excitement of the women when the king re-enters Kalyāṇa—a palpable effort to rival Kālidāsa—and the king is credited with a lengthy description of the monsoon (XIII), whether justly or no. The pleasures of the cool season are described in XVI; the king slays lions, pursues boars with hounds, and shoots arrows at the deer. The last canto is in many respects the most interesting; true to the tradition of the *Harṣacarita*, which is followed also in the *Gaüḍavaha*, despite its slight pretensions to a historical character, Bilhaṇa devotes it to an account of himself and his family and the kings of his land, as well as of his experiences in his wanderings.

Bilhaṇa is no mean poet; at the best he is a master of simple graphic description; the account of the death of Āhavamalla from an incurable fever, in the absence of his son, is told with picturesque and pathetic vigour (IV, 45–65). 'I know,' says the dying king, 'that my life, mobile as the end of the elephant's ear, is spent; confidence have I none save in him that is the lord of Pārvatī's life; it is my will to lay aside this delusion of the bodily life in the lap of the Tuṅgabhadrā with my thought set on Śiva,' and he fulfils duly this purpose. On the whole Bilhaṇa's diction is simple and clear, being content with the simpler plays on words and alliterations; it avoids as a rule long compounds, and is a quite reasonably accurate example of the Vaidarbha style, extolled by the theory, but in the main neglected in practice.

It is interesting and probably significant that the greatest historian who ever wrote in Sanskrit was also a native of

Kashmir. Kalhaṇa, who wrote in the middle of the twelfth century A.D., was the son of a Brahmin statesman who was involved in the fall of the king Harṣa, and the poet himself seems not to have enjoyed royal favour, whence may be explained the comparatively unbiased judgments of his work. The task he essays in the *Rājataraṅgiṇī*[1] is a great one, a complete history of Kashmir, whose geographical conditions had made it for many centuries a land by itself, contemptuous of foreigners. In the early part of the work we see the influence of the *Nīlamata Purāṇa*,[2] which contained the fabled tradition of early times and which Kalhaṇa sometimes verbally follows. The period from the advent of Aśoka to power was a vital one in the history of Kashmir, but all that we have recorded that is historical is his existence and his faith; his date is out by a millennium, and of his historical feats nothing is left. The Turuṣka kings mark the second great historical episode for Kashmir; again we have names, their foreign origin, and a chronology which misplaces them by 400 years in relation to Aśoka. The poet consults, indeed, in his effort to reproduce the past, old inscriptions on buildings erected by kings, but he has none of the spirit which the genius of Hekataios introduced, however imperfectly, into Greek historiography.[3] He accepts as genuine the marvellous, which Hekataios rejected as laughable; a father may reign 700 years after his son, or a king for 300 years; a queen may be divine and make her exit in the shape of a bee, and the intervention of demons is all in the day's work.

The duty of Kalhaṇa as he conceives it is that of a poet; it is a poet who must be a historian, for he alone has the power to present to the world the facts in such a way as to reveal that he possesses genius and insight. As a poet the work must have a dominant sentiment, 'Things come into being,' says the poet, 'in a moment they are destroyed; the sentiment of resignation presides like a sovereign over this work.' Kalhaṇa gazes over the history of his country, he sees all that is sad and dreary in it, and he encourages in himself

[1] Ed. M. A. Stein, Bombay, 1892; trs. London, 1900.

[2] Ed. *Punjab Sanskrit Series*, No. V.

[3] Cf. U. von Wilamowitz-Moellendorff, *Greek Historical Writing* (1908).

and in his readers the sentiment that recognises, and by recognition rises superior to, the vanity of human aims. He seeks, therefore, every artistic mode to set things vividly before us; as with Thukydides he places speeches in the mouths of this characters, which represent the thoughts they should have entertained, and he expounds in the form of a soliloquy their inmost motives. His characterisation in the main, like that of Bilhaṇa, lacks depth; goodness to perfection, though rare, vies with incredible evil; the noble prince pleads the cause of an oppressed people with a cynical king, who sneeringly preaches unlimited egoism; the politician or the soldier speaks pages of the text-books; they are not human beings, but rather poets, moralists, persons of such a drama as the *Mudrārākṣasa*, or the wise ape or jackal of the Indian fable. Nonetheless, Kalhaṇa knows well the types which thronged the petty principalities of his day, the rival ministers, the greedy soldiers, the intriguing priests, the teachers only too proficient in immorality, the untamed barons of the country, the frail ladies from the temples, and the royal *entourage* divided into hostile factions. He is a master of the petty politics of Kashmir, of its treachery, massacres, intrigue, murder, suicide, strife of son against father, of brother against brother, its worthless debauchees of kings, its intriguing queens like the bloodthirsty and lascivious Diddā (A.D. 980–1003), who put her own grandson to death in order to rule alone. It is to be set to his credit also that he recognises the difficulty of estimating character; the multitude of impressions flowing in upon the mind confuses the issue; he insists also that he is bound to give as true and impartial a verdict as a judge himself. But Kalhaṇa has too little insight to read effectively the complex mind and character of man, which forbid simple pronouncements, so intermingled are good and bad in all human hearts. Moreover, a serious hindrance in the way of fuller understanding is presented by his naïve belief in the power of evil omens, of hostile magic, of the intervention of demons, and above all, of the past deeds of man's long series of lives; 'what neither dream nor the juggler's art could produce, springs up, the marvel of mysterious working from the dark depths of ancient deeds.' As usual in Indian thought, beside the rule of the act begetting its sequence in a distant future stands the more easily intelligible, if logically irreconcilable, conception of fate. This idea looms large with Kalhaṇa; it is the power that pulls the strings of the puppets of the human stage; it intervenes to bring doubt and discomfiture into the clearest mind. The sun brings out the beauty of the lotus, but fate casts it under the feet of the elephant whose trunk uproots it from its place. On such a view it was impossible to seek a clear intelligence and appreciation of historical events, and Kalhaṇa makes no such effort; his aim is not to understand the course of events or predict the future; it is to inculcate by his great poem the feeling of the vanity of everything save resignation. For this end he applies all the resources of the Indian art of poetics and his large and recondite vocabulary, enriched by many local terms. Similes are used at every turn; the sun, the moon, the Himālaya, the Ganges, the lotus are pressed into constant play; and paronomasias abound. The hospital built by a pious queen becomes the cage for the swan of her good works. Or again, 'Princes and fishes when their thirst is excited by riches and impure water respectively, leave their place and fall into evil ways, and as a result are brought into the ineluctable net of death, the former by the dictates of fate, the latter by troops of fishermen.' This to us is more clever than pretty, but there is often very real power and vividness in Kalhaṇa's descriptions, as in the picture of the flight of prince Bhoja in A.D. 1144 to the country of the Dards:

> The points of icy rock encompassed him like the teeth of death; like the net of destruction the dark night of the clouds surrounded him; like herds of elephants snowdrifts flung their weight against him; the spray of the waterfalls smote his body like arrowshots; the skin, that guards the blood, burst open beneath the force of the drifting storm; his eyes were blinded by the glitter of the sun on the snowfields.

Kalhaṇa may not be a great historian, nor indeed does he rise above the rank of a chronicler, though one of poetic skill, but he is a happy contrast to the dreariness of the virtuous but dull Jaina monk, Hemacandra (A.D. 1088–1172), who has left among his voluminous works a *Dvyāśrayakāvya*, 20 cantos in Sanskrit and 8 in Prākrit, which serves the double purpose of illustrating the rules of grammar and celebrating his patron Kumārapāla of Aṇhilvāḍ and his predecessors.

Hemacandra was too much of a partisan to be an impartial or reliable historian, and too deplorably unpoetical to be a tolerable writer, but doubtless he felt no concern save to afford effective illustrations of his own grammatical lucubrations.[1] and to depict the ideal of a Jain monarch.

[1] Cf. G. Bühler, *Ueber das Leben des Jaina Mönches Hemachandra* (1889); ed. *Bombay Sanskrit Series*, Nos. 60, 69 and 76.

VI

THE PROSE ROMANCE AND THE CAMPŪ

NOTHING illustrates more clearly the defects in our tradition than the absence of any early specimens of the prose romance. We are confronted with the works of Daṇḍin, Subandhu, and Bāṇa without any remains of the many texts which must have preceded them to enable them to attain in their own diverse manners results so finished. The situation is precisely as in the case of the epic; the Brahmanical predecessors of Kālidāsa have almost entirely perished, leaving his perfect achievement to stand by itself; the fame of the later poets so completely eclipsed their forerunners that incurious generations allowed even their names to pass into oblivion. It is true that Bāṇa refers to Bhaṭṭāra Haricandra as the author of a prose composition of high merit; we do not, however, know anything further of this writer, who was manifestly not the author of the dull *Dharmaśaramābhyudaya*,[1] an epic on the saint Dharmanātha in verse of a wooden type, which imitates Māgha. We cannot, moreover, hail him as the creator of the prose of romance, which must have been gradually evolved under the influence of the poetic Kāvya during a considerable period of time.

The date of Daṇḍin is still a matter hotly contested.[2] There is no real ground for suggesting error in the traditional ascription to him of the *Kāvyādarśa* on poetics and

[1] Ed. *Kāvyamālā*, No. 8, 1888. Not before A.D. 900.

[2] H. Jacobi, *Sitzungsber. d. Preussischen Akademie*, 1922, pp. 210 ff.; Hari Chand, *Kālidāsa*, pp. 78 ff.; K. P. Trivedi, *Ind. Ant.*, xlii, 261; A.B. Gajendragadkar, *Daśakumāracarita*, pp. xxxiii ff.; Pathak, *Ind. Ant.*, xli, 235; xliv, 278; *J.B.R.A.S.*, xxiii, 29 f.; S. K. De, *Sanskrit Poetics*, i, 58 ff. Cf. chap. x.

the *Daśakumāracarita*; the fact that in the latter he offends against good taste and the rules of his own treatise is certainly not a ground for denying identity of authorship; it is much easier to preach than to practise, nor is it at all certain that he would have admitted that his practice actually ran counter to his doctrine. The tradition which assigns him a third work has caused needless conjectures; we may be certain that the missing book was not the *Mṛcchakaṭikā*, for the verse whose occurrence in the *Kāvyādarśa* and that play gave rise to Pischel's conjecture[1] has turned out to be taken bodily from Bhāsa's *Cārudatta*. The claim that the third work was the *Chandoviciti* is also dubious,[2] for Daṇḍin's reference to that text may be merely to the Chandaḥśāstra and not to a special text. That he was a southerner is suggested, but not proved, by his references to the Kaliṅgas, Andhras, Colas, and the banks of the Kāverī, as well as by his exaltation of the merits of the Vaidarbha style, while a reference has been suspected in the *Kāvyādarśa* to the Pallavas of Kāñcī.

The evidence for the poet's date is disappointingly confusing. The relation between him and the writer on poetics, Bhāmaha, has excited strong controversy without affording material for a convincing conclusion, as in our ignorance of the details of the progress of the theory of poetics we are often at a loss to know whether views of Daṇḍin are directed against Bhāmaha or against a predecessor whose opinions later were adopted by Bhāmaha. Again Bhāmaha's own date is dubious, although it was doubtless before the second half of the eighth century, when Vāmana flourished. Definite efforts have been made to prove that Daṇḍin used the *Bhaṭṭikāvya*, which contains illustrations of rhetorical figures, but, even assuming the completeness of the proof, the date of that Kāvya is not finally established. Further, references by Daṇḍin both to the *Harṣacarita* and the *Kādambarī* have been suggested, but in neither case with any cogency. What is moderately clear is that the style and the references to political divisions in India suggest a date not later than say

[1] Still maintained in *Die orientalischen Literaturen*, p. 206.

[2] Jacobi, *Ind. Stud.*, xvii, 447. An *Avantisundarīkathā* by a Daṇḍin (Dakṣiṇa Bhāratī Series, No. 3, 1924) appears to me to have no real claim to be by the author of the *Daśakumāracarita*, and, therefore, to yield no evidence of date.

A.D. 600 and possibly earlier. Efforts to make use of the king Rājavarman or Rātavarman's name as fixing a date in the seventh century must be deemed unproved and implausible.

The *Daśakumāracarita* reveals to us the graces of the Kāvya style applied to the folk tale, vivified by the genius of the writer. We have a vague parallel for the process in the *Satyra* of Petronius or in the picaresque romance. The folk tale we may assume as current in Prākrit, but we must be content to guess from the Sanskrit Kathās which are preserved to us, and which will later occupy our attention, what measure of development it had reached. What is certain from the available evidence is that it had never attained any of the elaboration which is shown in an incipient condition in Daṇḍin and as matured in Subandhu and Bāṇa. From the point of view of style the predecessor of the romance is not the tale, but the prose style which is manifested in the Grinar inscription of Rudradāman and Hariṣeṇa's panegyric of Samudragupta. That style is presented to us in its development in Bāṇa's *Harṣacarita*, and we may with reason hold that it was first applied in the historical story and then transferred to embellish the folk tale. This seems to lie at the base of the distinction between Ākhyāyikā and Kathā, which is presented to us in a puzzling confusion in the writers of poetics, explaining and justifying in large measure the refusal of Daṇḍin in his *Kāvyādarśa* to have anything to do with the distinction. If we accepted the view of the theorists[1] the distinction would largely turn on the fact that the Ākhyāyikā possesses divisions called Ucchvāsas, contains verses in Vaktra and Aparavaktra here and there, and is narrated by the hero, while the Kathā lacks these marks. Much more significant is the distinction,[2] which is also suggested, that the Ākhyāyikā rests on tradition, the Kathā on fancy; we may here have a vague recollection of the original distinction between the serious story in Sanskrit and the folk tale in Prākrit, to which the manner of the former was applied, as was inevitable,[3] in due course. The

[1] Bhāmaha, i, 25–9; contrast Daṇḍin, i, 23–30.

[2] Amarasiṁha, i, 5, 6. Lacôte (*Mélanges Lévi*, p. 269) makes the Kathā a complex Ākhyāyikā.

[3] Ānandavardhana (p. 143) allows longer compounds in the Ākhyāyikā than the Kathā.

views of the later theorists in general are plainly based on the view that the *Harṣacarita* is an example of the Ākhyāyikā, the *Bṛhatkathā* of the Kathā.

The *Daśakumāracarita* shares the peculiarity of both Bāṇa's romances in being unfinished and it is also, as we have it, a patchwork. The title tells us that we are to expect accounts of the adventures of ten princes; eight of these are given in the eight Ucchvāsas which make up the work proper; a Pūrvapīṭhikā in five Ucchvāsas supplies the history of two more as well as the framework, and an Uttarapīṭhikā completes the tale of Viśruta left incomplete in the last Ucchvāsa of the main text. Both the prelude and the supplement are extant in varied forms, which is enough to show that neither is Daṇḍin's, a view proved as regards the prelude by its definite divergence in some matters of note from the main body of the work. Even in the usual prelude the fifth Ucchvāsa is so much superior in style to the other four chapters as to suggest a different hand. We are clearly here in the presence of efforts to complete in Daṇḍin's style an imperfect masterpiece. As we have it, the framework is simple; the king of Magadha, defeated by the lord of Mālava, takes refuge in the Vindhya; his wife bears him a son, the young prince Rājavāhana. There are brought to the monarch in succession nine hapless sons of nobles and valiant but unfortunate kings, and the young princes grow up together. In due course they set out to win their fortune in the world, when they are met by one, in dress a Brahmin, but otherwise a Kirāta, who tells a strange story. Like his fellows, he had been a robber and murderer until one day he bade them spare a Brahmin; for this offence he was beaten and left for dead, but, though he descended to Yama's realm, he was spared for his humanity and permitted, after viewing the horrors of the realms below, to return to the world so that he might expiate his sins by reform. By penance he wins from Śiva the promise of the lordship of the world beneath, if he carry out the instructions graven on a copper plate at the foot of a deep grotto; for this end he asks the aid of a prince, and Rājavāhana at once accompanies him. Together they read the mandate, and by magic rites evoke the beautiful daughter of the king of the demons, whose marriage to the Kirāta follows. The grateful lover gives the prince a magic jewel which appeases hunger, thirst and suffering; he returns to the world with it, to find his comrades gone; ultimately all are reunited, each with a tale to recount. And curious the stories are; we are in a world of wonder, where the practical communism of the expert thieves in a few months turns the millionaires into beggars and *vice versâ*; where men can fall from the air into the arms of a stroller and harm neither themselves nor their unwilling host; where the rope that binds the captive changes into a beautiful girl, not reluctant to exchange the form of contact with the prisoner; where a magician carries away a lovely maiden to immolate her; where the thieves are experts in the art and possess complete burgling apparatus for the piercing of walls, where Buddhist nuns serve as go-betweens for courtesans, or help an injured wife to punish her husband, or are asked to aid in brutal seductions. Love here appears in its lightest and most passionate form as an affair of the senses; the hero shows his portrait to his emissary, bids him exhibit it to the maiden, and she will at once ask if the world really contain a person so beautiful; love at first sight, love which demands fulfilment without delay and despises every obstacle, is the normal motif, and in detail the pictures of love pleasure are often such as to evoke censure even from Indian critics.

Not Daṇḍin alone, however, but Subandhu himself has evoked Western censure by reason of what Professor Peterson styled his 'indecent puns' and Dr. F. Hall denounced as 'indelicacy,' which he attributed wholesale to Sanskrit literature. We have here, it is plain, a confusion of morality and literature, and the ignoring of the diverse standards of conduct of the West and mediæval India. The West, under the influence of Christianity, has come to accept monogamy, to demand purity from man and woman without distinction of class, and to deprecate any intimate description of personal beauty or of the joys of physical love. The code of Subandhu and Daṇḍin's day approved polygamy, respected and regulated the art of the courtesan, and as a natural outcome took pleasure both in vivid and detailed enumeration of the loveliness of women and the delights of conjugal felicity. To condemn the author because he accepted the moral standard and the literary taste, which accompanied it, is unjust, and it is idle to deny that the literary taste of the West is essentially bound up with its moral views. It may fairly be said that the moral outlook and social customs of India lessened the possibility of depicting the beauty of a pure, tender and spiritual affection ripening into passion, such as we find in modern literature, but on the other hand we find less stress laid on the painful and ignoble motif of the temptation to break the marriage vow. There is, indeed, both in Daṇḍin and in Subandhu actual departure at times from good taste, which is as censurable on Indian theory as on Western, but in Aśvaghoṣa and Kālidāsa himself the harem scenes are marked by traits which may be condemned from the standpoint of Western moral ideals, but cannot be condemned as literature, for they conform to the standard of æsthetic beauty.

Nothing illustrates better both Daṇḍin's divergence of moral outlook from the Western and his style than the advice given by an ascetic to the fair courtesan who, despite the entreaties of her mother, in love for a youth desires to abandon her calling and retire to the waste to practise holy living:

> Consider, my dear child, that life in the forest is difficult and painful. Those who adopt it expect as recompense either deliverance from rebirth or celestial bliss. But deliverance is hard to achieve; it falls to the lot only of the few who have perfect understanding. Heaven, it is true, all may gain, but the primary condition for the aspirant is to perform faithfully the duties of his station. Abandon then thy foolish enterprise, and live according to the desire of thy good mother.

Beside interesting glimpses of the under-world of his time, Daṇḍin has the merit of descriptive power in more normal regions of art; the advent of spring, the sunset, the sleeping posture of Ambālikā, the meeting of Rājavāhana and Avantisundarī have been justly singled out as admirable. Daṇḍin's style is still saved from the fatal effects of elaboration; in the main his prose is reasonably simple, clear and elegant, though occasionally his compounds, contrary to the rules of the Vaidarbha style to which he may be assigned, are too long, and the complication of the grammatical structure, with the suspension of the governing word, renders his exposition obscure or even deviates into incorrectness. His metaphors and similes are in the main effective and pretty; he is generally free from the obscure allusions, complex puns, involved constructions and exaggeration which disfigure the works of Bāṇa and Subandhu. But he is none the less a master of style; Ucchvāsa VII presents us with a brilliant *tour de force*, happily motived; it contains no labial sounds at all; Mantragupta the narrator, had been bitten so fiercely in the lip by his beloved that he avoided labials aud kept his lotus hand before his mouth as he spoke. In the Pūrvapīṭhikā we find alliteration and rime freely and indeed excessively employed with disregard to natural word-order, and occasionally syntactical and grammatical errors; these are rare in the genuine parts of the work in which Daṇḍin rather shows his skill in observing the rules of grammar, such as those respecting the use of the perfect in narrative. An ancient criticism assigns to Daṇḍin *padalālitya*, which may denote beauty of words and elegance of diction in general, and the praise is not undeserved by his cultivated, dignified, and correct diction, which often achieves melody and harmony of sound and sense.

Though Daṇḍin is not an easy writer, yet he is simplicity itself compared to Subandhu, who shares with him uncertainty of date. It is certain that he is earlier than Bāṇa, who refers to the *Vāsavadattā* in the preface to the *Harṣacarita*, although the doubt expressed, but repented of by Professor Peterson, has been lately revived. Two of his puns seem decisive of the fact that he was a contemporary of Bāṇa and that that writer wrote somewhat later in the seventh century than normally believed. We have it said of a maiden, 'beautified by ornaments as an assembly of Buddhists by the Alaṁkāra (*bauddhasaṁgatim ivālaṁkārabhūṣitām*),' which a scholiast naturally[1] takes as an allusion to the *Bauddhasaṁgatyalaṁkāra* of the famous Dharmakīrti, and the phrase, 'revealing her beauty as the permanence of the Nyāya system has its essence in Uddyotakara (*nyāyasthitim ivoddyotakarasvarūpām*),' a plain allusion to the illustrious exponent of the logic of the Nyāya, who was in all likelihood a contemporary

[1] Contra, Lévi, *Bull. de l'Ecole Française d'Extrême Orient*, iii, 18.

of Dharmakīrti in the early part of the seventh century A.D.[1] None of the other evidence is by any means convincing.

Some controversy exists as to whether the work is to be styled an Ākhyāyikā or Kathā, but the discussion is otiose. It must really be ranked as a Kathā. The work is in prose with introductory verses and a few interpolated in the course of the narrative. The story is simple; prince Kandarpaketu dreams of a lovely maiden and sets out with his friend, Makaranda, to find her. In the Vindhya he overhears the excuses made by a husband bird to his mate to explain his late hours; at Pāṭaliputra there is a princess, Vāsavadattā, who has seen in a dream a youth, to find whom she has despatched her confidante. The lovers meet; but, as the king plans the immediate wedding of the princess, they fly on a magic steed to the Vindhya. In the morning, however, the prince awakens to find his love gone; maddened he would slay himself but for a voice that promises him reunion with his beloved one, and, after many weary months of search, he finds her in stone form and reanimates her by his touch. She tells her tale; she had, while two armies fought to win her for their chiefs, intruded into the garden of an ascetic who, with true lack of chivalry, cursed her to become a stone until found by her lover. We have here the usual Kathā elements, the popular beliefs in dreams, speaking birds, magic steeds and transformations, but the incident is unimportant; what the poet praises himself for is that he is 'a treasure house of cleverness in the composition of a work which has a pun in every syllable,' and his whole object is to exhibit this skill in the descriptions which the Kāvya theory demands of mountain, forest and stream, the seasons and the watches of the day and the night, the valour of the hero and the loveliness of the heroine.

The work has been compared not inaptly to one of India's temples, where the outline is lost under the amazing delicacy of traceries. The equivoke is possible, only because the author is a perfect model of the Gauḍa style, whose distinguishing features are the love for long compounds, the heaping

[1] Cf. L. Gray's trans., pp. 8 ff.; and Keith, *J.R.A.S.*, 1914, pp. 1102 ff. This view has been disputed, but not conclusively. Ed. Fitzedward Hall, Calcutta, 1859; a variant text, reprinted from the Madras ed., 1862, is given by Gray.

up of epithets, forcible and resonant sounds rather than smoothness and delicacy, alliteration, etymologising, and hyperbole. He displays a baffling acquaintance with all the lore of his day, which enables him to confound even his commentators by the subtlety of his mythological allusions and his references to facts of nature or human life, and he employs a varied and *recherché* vocabulary, and the most varied figures of sound and sense, but above all alliteration. The punning is incessant; it varies from the simplest form, as in 'Adorned with a beautiful throat and armlets, as the army of monkeys is with Sugrīva and Aṅgada (*vānarasenām iva Sugrīvāṅgadopaśobhitām*),' to the more subtle, yet intelligible, 'There was infidelity among only materialists, because there was no poverty (*nāstikatācārvākeṣu*),' and the quite detestable, 'Which has no planet, yet knows Venus and Jupiter, for it is free from theft and knows the essence of poetry (*agraheṇāpi kāvyajīvajñena*),' or 'Roots were plucked out only in the case of wormwood trees, for ascetics did not pluck out their eyes (*netrotpāṭanam munīnām*).' The paronomasias have been described as 'veritable gems of terseness and twofold appropriateness,' the melody and sesquipedalian majesty of the long, rolling compounds and the lulling music of the alliterations have been extolled, and there is justice in all these claims. But in far too many cases the puns are far-fetched and do actual harm to the context; the compounds are repeatedly only to be understood by patient investigation for an end wholly unworthy of the pains exacted; the alliterations become foolish jingles in which for the sake of sound sense disappears; and the descriptions are either packed with commonplaces or rendered unintelligible by far-fetched conceits. Most unjustly has the romance been paralleled in merit with the *Euphues* of Lyly, for, fond as is that author of antitheses, paronomasias, alliterations and forced mythological allusions, he is simplicity and naïveté itself compared to Subandhu. The Alexandrian[1] Lykophron offers a better parallel for evasive allusion, but the genius of the Greek language forbade the additional obscurity of the compounds, often ludicrously long and heaped up in long

[1] See U. von Wilamowitz-Moellendorff, *Hellenistische Dichtung* (1924).

and cumbrous sentences, full of epithets on epithets, which cease only when the author's ingenuity for the moment has exhausted itself and is recovering preparatory to a new flight. In Daṇḍin the sentiments of wonder, heroism, and above all love are allowed to emerge freely from the romance, but in Subandhu love and wonder alike are smothered beneath a mass of often unmeaning words.

Unluckily Bāṇa chose both in the *Kādambarī* and in the historical romance the *Harṣacarita* to vie with Subandhu,[1] and to obscure his natural powers, far superior to those of his predecessor, by the adoption of the same style. The *Kādambarī* differs from the *Harṣacarita* in that it has found a hand to complete it in the shape of his son, Bhūṣaṇa Bhaṭṭa, to whom the Uttarabhāga of the tale is due.[2] The story, admittedly a Kathā, is complex in construction, though it agrees with the *Daśakumāracarita* and the *Vāsavadattā* in the essential characteristic of enclosing narrative within narrative, which is a real feature of the Kathā, but one not explicitly recognised in the theory. It introduces us to a king Śūdraka, to whose Court comes a Caṇḍāla maiden with a parrot; the bird is induced to recite to the king its sad tale; like Bāṇa himself, it was reared by its father, who later perished cruelly; the young bird saved by the paternal devotion is comforted by the sage Jābāli, whose long story is solemnly repeated by the parrot. Tārāpīḍa, king of Ujjayinī, has a wife, Vilāsavatī, and a minister, Śukanāsa; by Śiva's favour the royal pair attain a son, Candrāpīḍa, and Śukanāsa a son, Vaiśampāyana; the two boys grow up in every virtue, living in a special hall built for them outside the city. When sixteen years old, they are brought back to the city. Candrāpīḍa is given a wonderful horse, Indrāyudha, and as a faithful companion Pattralekhā, daughter of a king taken captive by Tārāpīḍa and reared by the queen. A few days later Candrāpīḍa, who has already received counsels of statecraft from Śukanāsa, is dismissed on a conquest of the world as Yuvarāja, and for three years subdues the earth, capturing the Kirātas' stronghold on Hemakūṭa. One day in pursuit of two Kinnaras

[1] See *Vienna Oriental Journal*, i, 115 ff.; xii, 21 ff.; xv, 246 ff.

[2] Ed. P. Peterson, Bombay, 1883; trs. C. M. Ridding, London, 1896.

he leaves his followers, and, wearied of the vain quest, finds by a lake a maiden, Mahāśvetā, doing penance. From her lips he hears her sad tale; how she met one Puṇḍarīka, loved and was loved, but the youth perished, while she hesitated to cast aside shame and maidenly duty and mate with him without her parents' leave; how she wished to die on her beloved's funeral pyre, but a divine figure snatched his body away and promised her reunion. From the maiden Candrāpīḍa learns of her friend Kādambarī, meets her, is enamoured and is loved in return, but at his father's call goes back to Ujjayinī before the lovers, in their shy reticence, have assured themselves directly of their mutual passion.

Bāṇa's work ends abruptly with the report made to Candrāpīḍa by Pattralekhā, who has come to assure him of Kādambarī's devotion. The continuation shows us Candrāpīḍa at last ready to seek his beloved, but ill fortune comes; he sets out to meet Vaiśampāyana, who was to bring his host to Ujjayinī, but finds that the hero has disappeared, having insisted on staying on the banks of the lake where Mahāśvetā dwells. The prince returns to the city, where the king blames him for Vaiśampāyana's loss, and the minister censures his son; at last he is despatched to seek his comrade: he finds no one at the lake but Mahāśvetā, who in tears tells of a Brahmin boy who sought her love, which faithful to Puṇḍarīka, she denied, and, when he pressed her, cursed him to become a parrot, whereupon he fell lifeless. The news breaks Candrāpīḍa's heart; he falls, dead to all seeming, and at this moment Kādambarī arrives to mingle her tears with those of Mahāśvetā. A divine voice comforts them, reassures Mahāśvetā of reunion with Puṇḍarīka, and bids them preserve the dead body of Candrāpīḍa which had lost the soul through a curse. Pattralekhā and Indrāyudha enter the lake, and there emerges Kapiñjala, the companion of Puṇḍarīka when he died, who tells the maidens the truth; Candrāpīḍa is an incorporation of the moon, Vaiśampāyana was Puṇḍarīka, and Indrāyudha Kapiñjala. The body is tended, remaining intact, and Tārāpīḍa and his consort come to live near it. The parrot now continues the tale in his own words, for by Jābāli's narrative he has recognised his true self as Puṇḍarīka-Vaiśampāyana. He determines to seek Candrāpīḍa, but is captured *en route* by a Caṇḍāla and given to his queen. She is no other than the Caṇḍāla maid who has brought the parrot. Questioned by Śūdraka, she reveals to him his true nature as Candrāpīḍa and disappears. The king dies, and simultaneously Kādambarī finds Candrāpīḍa reviving in her arms. Puṇḍarīka comes beside them; the nuptials are celebrated and complete happiness prevails at Ujjayinī and Hemakūṭa alike.

This is a strange and complex story, but in the main it is no invention of Bāṇa's; there is conclusive evidence[1] that he took it from the *Bṛhatkathā* of Guṇāḍhya, and that his chief work was to alter in detail and heighten the artistic merits of the tale. But, even as it is altered, it suffers grave disadvantage from the retention of the boxing of tale within tale. The absurdity of putting the major part of the tale in a parrot's mouth is irritating, and Śūdraka is a mere lay figure, which might well have been dispensed with. But there is distinct merit in the device by which the love of Mahāśvetā is set off against that of Kādambarī; the double thread of the narratives of the loves of the two maidens is skilfully interlaced; the peace of the life of the birds in their haunt and the hermits in their abode is admirably contrasted with the glories of the Courts of Śūdraka and Tārāpīḍa. The outstanding merit of the tale is unquestionably the painting of the emotion of love in the person of Kādambarī, with her alternation between her new passion and shame, hope and despondency, filial duty and longing for her lover, and her deep and abiding sorrow when death seems to remove him and to leave her nothing save the insecure hope of a distant reunion. We may justly complain that the hindrances to the fruition of her love are unnatural and unreal, for there is no adequate reason against an open wooing, and the confusion of curses and changing personalities is wearisome. But none the less Bāṇa has a real mastery over the emotions of love, free from grossness, and pathos; he can bring home to us the mystery of the affection which lives beyond death and craves for a reunion which the doctrine of transmigration rendered it possible to gratify. Nor is his power limited to this aspect of life only; the advice of Śukanāsa to Candrāpīḍa

[1] Cf. *Kathāsaritsāgara*, lix, 22 ff.; L. von Mankowski, *Vienna Or. Journal*, xv, 213–50; *Bṛhatkathāmañjarī*, xvi, 183 ff.

is an admirable discourse on practical politics, and there are throughout happy pieces of vigorous and picturesque description. Moreover, the minor characters are effectively drawn, the noble Tārāpīḍa who lays aside his own grief for the sake of another, the loving and timorous Vilāsavatī, the clever and upright minister, and the devoted Pattralekhā are all made real and living. His eye for the bizarre is manifested in the description of a Draviḍa ascetic seen by Candrāpīḍa at a shrine of Durgā, though the length of the digression to describe his antics is excessive and unartistic.[1]

Nevertheless, the demerits of Bāṇa as a stylist are deplorable. Indian critics indeed admire him; Kavirāja celebrates Subandhu, Bāṇa, and himself as incomparable in double entendres (*vakrokti*), and with the poetess Śīlābhaṭṭārikā he is made out to be a master of the Pāñcāla style, in which sense and sound are to be of equal importance.[2] His power of suggestion (*dhvani*) is said to silence all other poets. What we do find is the construction of vast sentences —extending even to six pages of print—the construction held in suspense until the end, and the whole eked out by the heaping of epithet on epithet in long compounds, diversified here and there by short sentences, like oases in a desert of words. Or, as Weber has it, Bāṇa's prose is an Indian wood where the undergrowth must be cut away to render a passage possible, and wild beasts in the shape of unknown words lie in wait for the wayfarer. His love of far-fetched allusions is inseparable from the punning, and his allusions to flora and fauna are exhaustive, and, to the reader exhausting, while, like Subandhu, he is a master of intricate mythology. The jingle of assonances he affected almost as much as Subandhu. It may be amusing to read that 'The beaks of parrots were red, but not faces with anger; the points of Kuśa grass were sharp, but not men's natures; the plantain leaves were fickle, but not men's minds,' but when this runs on indefinitely and includes 'There was destruction of the hairs of ascetics (*munibālanāśa*) in the ritual of consecration, not of their children by death,' and 'There was the killing of Śakuni in

[1] Cf. Peterson's *Kādambarī*, pref., and P. V. Kane's ed. (1920).
[2] See P. V. Kane, *Kādambarī*, p. xxv.

the *Mahābhārata*, but not of birds in the hermitage,' the whole thing rapidly becomes wearisome.

Of Bhūṣaṇa Bāṇa we need only say that he is decidedly inferior in fancy, in mythological ingenuity, and in knowledge of flora and fauna to his father, while, though he needlessly protracts the description of Kādambarī's love sorrow, he hastens on the story somewhat inartistically to its *dénouement.* But in the main he falls little short of Bāṇa himself in his command of language and perverted ingenuity.

Despite the fame of Bāṇa, his example does not seem to have been often followed, though his fondness for puns aided the poets of the inscriptions to enrich their pedestrian topics. We have, however, in the *Tilakamañjarī*[1] of Dhanapāla, who enjoyed the patronage of the Court of Dhārā and wrote the *Pāiyalacchi*, a Prākrit vocabulary and the *Ṛṣabhapañcāśikā* in honour of the Jain saint, a close imitation of the style and manner of the *Kādambarī* in the account of the love of the heroine, who gave her name to the tale and Samaraketu. Bāṇa's influence is also marked in the *Gadyacintāmaṇi*[2] of the Jain Oḍayadeva Vādībhasiṁha, which is a life of the mythic Jīvandhara and of uncertain date.

There has been raised in connection with the romance the question whether in this respect India is not indebted to the West.[3] The romance, it is contended, as it appears in the *Kādambarī*, in distinction from the *Bṛhatkathā*, is a development so marked as to require or render probable the suggestion of external models affecting Indian taste. The model is found in the Greek romance; Achilles Tatius has passages which in their description of womanly beauty, in their fondness of drawing parallels from love among animals and even plants, and in their general tenor are strongly suggestive of the ideas of Bāṇa in the *Kādambarī*. Moreover, it is admitted that Greek astrology affected powerfully Indian astrology and astronomy, nor is there any reason *a priori* why the influence should not have gone further than a technical science. The weakness of the theory may be sufficiently

[1] Ed. Bombay, 1903.

[2] Ed. Madras, 1902; his *Kṣatracūḍāmaṇi* is also ed. there 1903. Cf. *Z.D.M.G.*, lxviii, 697 f.

[3] Peterson, *Kādambarī*, pp. 101 ff.; Rohde, *Der griech. Roman*, pp. 578 ff.; Reich, *Deutsche Literaturzeitung*, 1915, pp. 553 ff.

demonstrated by its history. Posed in this form by Professor Peterson, it received a new shape at the hands of M. Lacôte,[1] who sought to show that the *Bṛhatkathā* itself was affected by Greek literature, that the idea of a romance and the plan of his work have been taken thence by Guṇāḍhya. The *Marvels Beyond Thyle* of Antonius Diogenes is a tale of love and marvellous travel; Lucian, who parodies it in his *True History*, mentions a race of aerial beings who are like the Vidyādharas of the *Bṛhatkathā*; the *Babylonika* of Iamblichos narrates how the hero, Rhodanes, persecuted along with his wife by the king of Babylon, finally, after many strange adventures, becomes king in the room of his enemy. In Xenophon of Ephesos we have the two lovers, Habrokomes and Antheia, separated immediately after their marriage, and united only after many moving experiences, as in the *Bṛhatkathā* is the fate of Naravāhanadatta and Madanamañjukā. Moreover, it was pointed out that the Yavanas appear in the *Bṛhatkathā* as artists, as excellent makers of couches, and even of aerial machines, an idea reminding us of the fame of the treatise on mechanics of Heron of Alexandria. The value of this evidence may be accurately gauged when it is added that on further consideration M. Lacôte[2] came to the precisely opposite conclusion, that the Greek romance was borrowed from the Indian. To investigate this claim would involve a needless incursion into the field of the Greek romance, but it is important to recognise that there are parallels between the romance in Greece and India but also substantial divergence, which shows adequately the essential independence of these products of two different civilisations and literatures, that of India and that of Asiatic Greece.

It was almost inevitable that the prose form of the romance should come to be freely diversified by verse, as an additional ornament, especially as this type of composition was already current in the fable literature and the influence of the poetic Kāvya was always present. But we have no early instance of this type. The first works preserved to us are of the tenth century. The Nausari grant of Indra III, the Rāṣṭrakūṭa, of A.D. 915 gives us the date of Trivikrama

[1] *Le Bṛhatkathā*, pp. 284 ff.
[2] *Mélanges Lévi*, pp. 249 ff. See Keith, *J.R.A.S.*, 1915, pp. 784 ff.

Bhaṭṭa, who wrote the *Damayantīkathā*[1] and a *Madālasacampū* in the new form of combined prose and poetry, which is recognised in the *Sāhityadarpaṇa* as legitimate in a Kathā, in order to increase, doubtless, the emotional effect in appropriate crises. The former work is imperfect; it is marked by all the defects of Bāṇa's style, endless epithets, long compounds, monstrous sentences, and constant puns, with overdone alliterative and rime effects, while the verses are commonplace and intricate. The work deserves mention merely as it illustrates with painful accuracy the defects of the manner in the hands of mediocrity.

More important is the Jain romance, the *Yaśastilaka*[2] of Somadeva, written, in A.D. 959, in the reign of the Rāṣṭrakūṭa Kṛṣṇa and his feudatory, a son of the Cālukya Arikesarin II. The story is interesting, though, as inevitable with a Jain, it has a missionary purpose. Māridatta, a Yodheya king, is induced to perform a sacrifice of two of every kind of things, including a boy and a girl; but, when an ascetic and his twin sister, really his nephew and niece, who had through insight into their past lives embraced the career of ascetics, are led before him, he suffers a change of heart, as had been planned by the Jain sage, Sudatta, in whose company the children had lived. He questions them, ascertains their identity, and in Āśvāsa II is entertained by the boy's account of his previous life as Yaśodhara, son of king Yaśortha or Yaśorgha and Candramatī. In Āśvāsa III he recounts his conversations with his ministers, who incidentally quote many stanzas from famous poets of old, and his conquests, which, however, are ruined by his wife's faithlessness. He first meditates slaying her, then adopting the ascetic life; his mother bids him sacrifice instead, but he inveighs against it as foolish and wicked, finally compromising on the offer of a cock of flour. The guilty wife solves their troubles by poisoning the offering so that both die. In Āśvāsa IV we hear of their repeated rebirths and fate until the mother and son are now the twins, who are determined to make an end of transmigration and advise the king to seek Sudatta's aid and achieve the same end, which is performed in the last four didactic chapters of the tale.

[1] Ed. *Kāvyamālā*, No. 85, 1903.
[2] Ed. *Kāvyamālā*, No. 70, 1901–3.

Bāṇa among others is quoted by the author, whose good taste and humour may be illustrated by a couple of his stanzas:

> Of feminine things age is most to be desired, for from her embrace men cease to covet the coquettish glances of others of her sex.
>
> What can instruction do for thee, that art at once learned and modest? What sane man would bring salt as offering to the sea?

There is, of course, no comparison between Bāṇa and his follower in brilliance, but the manner of boxing tale in tale and the introduction of the motif of transmigration is precisely in the manner of the *Kādambarī*.

Other Campūs are of uncertain date, such as the *Jīvandharacampū*[1] of Haricandra, who, we may be sure, is not the Haricandra of Bāṇa, who is doubtless the same as the author referred to along with Bhāsa, Kālidāsa and Subandhu by Vākpati. This work is clearly later than the ninth century. The *Rāmāyaṇacampū*, ascribed to Bhoja of Dhārā, is a most uninteresting text, doubtless much later than that king, and, still later, Campūs abound.

The origin of the literary form of the Campū and the romance has been traced[2] to a primitive narrative style, in which artless prose was combined with more elaborate verse, as in the Pāli *Jātakas*, the course of development being either the disappearance of the simple prose, which gives the epic poem, or the improvement of the artistic character of the prose to match the verse, as in the Campū, or, again, the verse is dismissed and we have the romance in prose. The theory, however, must be admitted to rest on very slender foundations. Of the narrative type in prose and verse postulated from the Vedic period downwards we have hardly any real examples, and the only genuine combination of verse and prose that seems to be early is the fable type with gnomic or recapitulatory verse, which bears a close similitude to the habit of the *Dharma Sūtras* to enforce rules by verse citations. The combination of prose and verse in narrative seems, as a matter of historical fact, to be most

[1] Ed. Tanjore, 1905. Perhaps also author of the *Dharmaśarmābhyudaya*.

[2] See Pischel, *Die orientalischen Literaturen*, p. 199; Oldenberg, *Zur Geschichte der altindischen Prosa* (1917); on the other side, Keith, *J.R.A.S.*, 1911, pp. 979 ff.; 1912, pp. 429 ff.; *Rigveda Brāhmaṇas*, pp. 63 ff.; Hertel *Vienna Or. Journ.*, xxiii, 285 ff.

easily understood as the natural result of the co-existence of two forms of literature dealing with the same subject[1] matter. The mixture of verse and prose in inscriptions, at any rate, is quite naturally thus explained, and, if the Campū is really a very old literary form, the historical connecting link between Vedic Ākhyānas of the prose-verse type postulated, it is curious that it appears so late in history, and that we have earlier by far both the verse and the prose narrative.[2]

[1] Seen in Hariṣeṇa's Praśasti (above, p. 27).

[2] Works of the *Jātakamālā* type (p. 101) represent in content and form a transition from the tale to the romance. Occasional instances in the *Mahābhārata* are doubtless cases of contamination, not relics of primitive form, as held by Oldenberg, *Das Mahābhārata*, pp. 21 ff. For later prose versions of verse originals in which verses and portions of verses appear, see J. Hertel, *Streitberg Festgabe*, p. 138 f. When verse is used, it naturally appears especially where there is a higher pitch of interest.

VII

THE POPULAR TALE

In the romance, such as the *Kādambarī*, we have seen the application of the Kāvya manner to the popular and relatively simple tale. We need not doubt that stories of the type of the Western fairy tale were long current among the people, and that the literary form which collections of these narratives first assumed was one in Prākrit[1] rather than Sanskrit, the language of the higher classes and of serious literary effort. This accords well with all that we know of the history of the literature. As the Sanskrit *Pañcatantra* or *Tantrākhyāyika* heads the history of the beast fable, through the perfecting of a new literary genre, so the *Bṛhatkathā*[2] of Guṇāḍhya, in Paiśācī Prākrit heads the literature of the tale. Its fame has, as usual, deprived us of knowledge of its predecessors.

A curious legend is all that is vouchsafed to us of the origin of this work; it is given in the *Kathāsaritsāgara* and the *Bṛhatkathāmañjarī* and in a variant form in the *Śloka-saṁgraha*. The essence of it is that the tales were written in Paiśācī by Guṇāḍhya after he had, as the result of a rash wager with Śarvavarman, who is the reputed author of the *Kātantra* grammar, debarred himself from the use of other languages. The locality of his labours is placed by the first two of these sources in the Vindhya, while his birth is assigned to Pratiṣṭhāna on the Godāvarī, where reigned a king, Sātavāhana, ignorant of Sanskrit and, therefore, put to shame by his wife who, tired of sporting in the bath, forbade him to splash her with water (*modakaiḥ*), a behest misunder-

[1] We may assume that it was never put in vernacular form; vernacular prose appears first in the nineteenth century.

[2] See F. Lacôte, *La Bṛhatkathā* (1908), and ed. of the *Śloka-saṁgraha*; F. D. K. Boseh, *de legende van Jimūtavāhana in de Sanskrit-Litteratuur* (1914).

stood by the monarch, through not knowing the rules of euphonic combination, as an order to pelt her with sweetmeats. The *Ślokasaṁgraha* places the poet's birth at Mathurā and his patron at Ujjayinī, but it must be admitted that it is clearly dominated by the desire to bring the poet to Nepal and, therefore, is inferior in value to the other sources, which, though of Kashmir, do not insert it in the story. It is important that Daṇḍin already knows that the work was written in the speech of Bhūtas, ghosts or demons, and, accordingly, must be assumed to have heard the legend in some form. The fame of the work is also attested by Subandhu, by Bāṇa's *Kādambarī* and by his *Harṣacarita*. Of what date it was is left wholly dubious; Sātavāhana is a dynastic name which may denote any of several kings, and the fact that the *Kātantra* grammar with Śarvavarman is introduced would suggest rather a later than an earlier date, for what evidence there is suggests that the Sātavāhanas were great patrons of the Prākrit literature, and can only gradually have come round to the necessity of accepting Sanskrit as the language of the Court.[1] It is, therefore, impossible to place Guṇāḍhya with any certainty before the fifth century A.D., unless we hold that Bhāsa (fourth century) derived from him, and not from tradition, some of his themes.

The language in which Guṇāḍhya wrote was Paiśācī, and, unless we are to disregard entirely the tradition, we must suppose that it was a dialect which he picked up in the Vindhya region. Not unnaturally, and in accordance with Indian tradition as preserved among others by Rājaśekhara in his *Kāvyamīmāṁsā*,[2] the view has been taken that the Prākrit is a literary version of a dialect of the Vindhyas. On the other hand, it has been drawn into the effort of Sir G. Grierson to establish a Paiśāca group of north-western languages, based on the theory that Paiśāca denoted a group of cannibal Aryan tribes. This part of the theory is clearly untenable; Paiśācī means, as tradition is accordant in holding, the language of demons. The question, whether a north-west Prākrit existed in Guṇāḍhya's time similar to the Prākrit which he used, is one which, in the absence of any

[1] Cf. Bloch, *Mélanges Lévi*, p. 15 f.

[2] P. 51; Konow, *J.R.A.S.*, 1921, p. 244 f. Grierson's reply (pp. 424 ff.) is ineffective.

adequate evidence, may be left aside; that he was not a north-westerner, but borrowed the dialect from Banyans from the Punjab or others, is clearly implausible. At any rate, what he wrote in, if we may trust the scanty fragments preserved and apparently taken from the *Bṛhatkathā*,[1] was a decidedly artificial form of speech; it hardened the *d* alone, and was clearly more closely related to Sanskrit that any average Prākrit. That it was ever used by any other genre of literature is most uncertain, for we cannot put any special faith in the late Buddhist tradition that the Sthaviras used Paiśācī for their scriptures.

Of the content of Guṇāḍhya's work we have somewhat remote knowledge from two main sources. The first is derived from Kashmir: the *Bṛhatkathāmañjarī* of Kṣemendra, the polymath, written about a quarter of a century before the *Kathāsaritsāgara* (more properly perhaps *Bṛhatkathāsaritsāgara*) of Somadeva, composed between A.D. 1063–66 and 1081–88, gives, as does Somadeva, a version of the *Bṛhatkathā*, which was formerly held to be taken directly from the original. This idea must now be discarded, both on internal evidence and because of the second source of knowledge now available, the *Slokasaṁgraha* of Budhasvāmin, a Nepalese work which, mainly on the score of the form of the author's name, has been assigned with moderate plausibility to the eighth or ninth century A.D. It is clear beyond doubt, although we have but a fragment of 28 chapters and 4,524 verses of the latter work, that the Kashmir texts are taken from a very different source than the *Bṛhatkathā* itself. There had grown up, it is plain, in Kashmir, probably by gradual evolution, a *Bṛhatkathā* which was based on an epitome of the original work, but into which much extraneous matter had been placed, including, as we shall see, a version of the *Pañcatantra*, foreign to the original. This re-fashioning of the *Bṛhatkathā* seems[2] to have been in the Paiśācī, and there is nothing implausible in this, for the rule that a literary

[1] It is, of course, perfectly possible that the fragments come from the Kashmirian version, and not from Guṇāḍhya at all.

[2] There is no strict proof; the dialect may have been modernised. It is strange that a public existed which cared for a Paiśācī rendering of the *Pañcatantra*, but our ignorance of the dialect renders it difficult to judge its merits.

speechform should be kept, once established, is attested for us by the stereotyped Prākrits of the drama which from Kālidāsa's day onwards are preserved for certain rôles. The date of the changes is wholly uncertain; there is no need to date it any great time before the gradual disuse of Paiśācī among other causes induced the translations into Sanskrit. The Nepalese version, on the other hand, seems to have adhered more closely to the original and to derive from it; the use of Sanskrit in this case is natural, for the civilisation received by Nepal from India was essentially Brahmanical.

We can gather, though indistinctly, some conception of the essential character of Guṇāḍhya's work, which was marked by a degree of originality decidedly beyond the average. The plan of his work, obscured in the Kashmirian versions by the addition of enormous masses of extraneous material, perhaps to the extent of nine-tenths of that version, was based on the scheme of the *Rāmāyaṇa*. Rāma there, with Lakṣmaṇa to aid him, recovers Sītā and at the same time the throne of his father. In the *Bṛhatkathā* Naravāhanadatta sets out first with Vegavatī, then, after being parted from her, with Gomukha, on a series of adventures which result in his attaining at once marriage with Madanamañjukā, or Madanamañcukā, and the empire of the Vidyādharas. As Sītā is preserved pure in the hands of Rāvaṇa, so Madanamañjukā keeps herself unharmed by her ravisher, Mānasavega. The influence of the Buddhist legend of the Cakravartin is also apparent; Naravāhanadatta is born with the established thirty-two marks, which signify that, if a boy forsake the life of the home, he will become a Buddha. But, if he remain in the secular life, he will achieve the rank of emperor. But the vital distinction between these traditions and Guṇāḍhya's conception is that in the latter the empire to be attained is not one over Kṣatriyas and Brahmins on the plains of India, but in the Himālayas over the Vidyādharas, a race which, all in all, is no more than a product of popular fancy based on the Gandharvas of the Veda, with both their attractive and fickle aspects, and the Yogins of Brahmanism, the Arhants of Buddhism. It is the fate of Naravāhanadatta, thanks to merit accumulated in bygone births, to gain the sevenfold magic science, which wins him the position he covets, and the tale of the *Bṛhatkathā* was the narrative of the course of his adventures. In keeping with the new orientation of ideas, the adventures are such as appeal to the merchant, the sailor, the worker; the great god is not Śiva or Viṣṇu, but Kubera, lord of riches. The heroic ideals of Brahmanism and Buddhism are brought down to the level of bourgeois life.

To Guṇāḍhya also is due the praise of creating effective and distinctive characters, in the shape of Naravāhanadatta himself, of Gomukha and of Madanamañjukā. The first is traced in his development from an attractive and ingenuous youth, a worthy child of the gay and amorous Udayana, through a certain decadence due to his good fortune and brilliant destiny, until as emperor he attains the summit of all desires, and is incapable of anything save justice. Gomukha has far more life and energy; he is a much more modern counterpart of the sage Yaugandharāyaṇa, counsellor of Udayana; unfailing in courage, resource, and power of turning every situation to the best advantage, he appears indomitable amid apparent adversity, even if his means to attain victory are more efficacious than honourable. Madanamañjukā is a character with only one parallel in Indian literature, the heroine of the *Cārudatta* and the *Mṛcchakaṭikā*. The daughter of a courtesan, therefore destined to follow the duty of her rank and caste, she, none the less, is inspired by a noble pride and seeks to be freed from the odious future, which presents itself as her duty, and to be married in legitimate fashion to Naravāhanadatta, a desire finally achieved. If we may assume that Madanamañjukā was the earlier conception, then we may find here a fairly satisfactory piece of evidence for placing the *Bṛhatkathā* not later than the early part of the fourth century A.D.[1] But this is wholly speculative. In the detail of the adventures of his hero we may be assured that Guṇāḍhya drew freely on the travellers' tales and the popular narratives of his day. For much of his account of Pradyota and Udayana we find parallels in the Vinaya of the Mūlasarvāstivādin school; both Kauśāmbī and Ujjayinī were clearly rich in legends of their princes.

[1] The date of the *Mṛcchakaṭikā* is very dubious; H. Jacobi, *Bhavisattakaha*, p. 83, n. 1; Keith, *Sanskrit Drama*, p. 128 f.

That Guṇāḍhya wrote in verse seems at first suggested by certain evidence, including the fact that the versions we have are in verse and the Kashmirian accounts seem clearly to assume a verse original. The evidence to the contrary is slight and not wholly conclusive; no great stress can be laid on the quotations of Hemacandra, whose actual knowledge of the original *Bṛhatkathā* is problematical, but the fact that Daṇḍin says that a Kathā is in prose and gives the *Bṛhatkathā* as a famous work, is much more important. It remains, of course, possible that it was partly in prose, partly in verse.[1]

Of the Sanskrit versions that of Budhasvāmin has high merits. The style is simple but elegant, and in harmony with the subject matter. Rarely does the author permit himself the luxury of ornamental description, usually an impulse irresistible by a Sanskrit poet. His characters are clearly and vividly drawn, far less conventionally than usual; he can paint a situation in a few well chosen words, and he imparts to his work that tone of lighthearted curiosity and interest in the world and its odd happenings which best suits the theme. His language is marked by the introduction of a number of Prākritisms, probably borrowed from the original; he is expert in Sanskrit grammar and readily uses in the Kāvya style rare constructions, among them a wealth of aorists.

No high praise can be given to Kṣemendra's work;[2] it has all the demerits of the other epitomes of the author; he is so anxious to abbreviate, and successful in the task, as he has only some 7,500 Ślokas against 22,000 of Somadeva, that he is quite indifferent to considerations of intelligibility and interest, and would often be wholly misleading if it were not for the possibility of adducing the fuller version of Somadeva. On the other hand, he loves, when he has the opportunity, to enter into descriptive divagations; he gladly avails himself of such occasions and displays his command of an agreeable and even elevated, if decidedly mannered, style. Somadeva, on the other hand, shows far better judgment and taste; he realises that elegances of style are out of place in

[1] There is no suggestion that it was in prose-poetry form. For its date, cf. Keith, *J.R.A.S.*, 1909, pp. 145 ff. Lacôte's suggestion of the first century A.D. (*Mélanges Lévi*, p. 270) is unsupported, unless Bhāsa used it.

[2] Ed. *Kāvyamālā*, No. 69.

his task of simple and vivid narrative, and, as he certainly possessed the power to vie with Kṣemendra, his self-restraint merits full recognition as extremely rare in later Indian literature. The flow of his narrative is normally clear and easy; he is capable of very diverse effects, from the amusing episode of the sensitive man who felt so keenly through seven mattresses a single hair that he was robbed of sleep to the affecting tale of king Śibi or the elaborate love adventures of the hero; his language and metre show a certain carelessness as opposed to the precision in the best Kāvyas, but this is neither unnatural nor open to censure in the tale. As opposed to Kṣemendra, he preserves better the main narrative into which the other tales are fitted and from which the work derives its style, *Kathāsaritsāgara*, the ocean of the streams of stories.[1]

The work is divided into 18 Lambhakas, with 124 Taraṅgas, billows, the latter division an innovation of Somadeva's. Book I gives the tale of Guṇāḍhya, under the style of Kathāpīṭha; II narrates the history of Udayana as the Kathāmukha, the basis of the tale; in III we have the story of the winning by him of Padmāvatī, the title Lāvāṇaka being derived from the place in which Vāsavadattā was reputed to have perished by fire; in IV we reach the birth of Naravāhanadatta, the true hero. In Book V we have a new motif, introduced by the slender connecting link of the desire on the part of the Vidyādhara prince, Śaktivega, to see the emperor to be; he recounts how he himself reached the marvellous city of the Vidyādharas and espoused four maidens, a fact which gives the book its name, Cāturdārika. We learn here of the marvellous birds, the rocs of the Arabs, who bear the wanderer to the city of wonders. In VI, which bears the title, Madanamañcukā, Naravāhanadatta is unexpectedly introduced as telling the tale of his own adventures after he has become emperor, a sign doubtless of the confusion of the Kashmirian *Bṛhatkathā*. We have a series of Buddhist tales, then a long narrative of the love adventures of Kaliṅgasenā, whom Udayana would have married but for Yaugandharāyaṇa's intrigues, and whose daughter, Madanamañcukā, is destined

[1] Ed. Bombay, 1889; trs. C. H. Tawney, Calcutta, 1880–84; reprinted with additions by N. M. Penzer, London, 1924–27; Speyer, *Studies about the Kathāsaritsāgara* (1908).

for Naravāhanadatta. In VII we have two entirely different motifs; the first is that which gives the book its title, Ratnaprabhā, the marriage of Naravāhanadatta with the daughter of a Vidyādhara king who comes to visit him; the second shows us the prince setting out to the camphor land beyond the sea, together with Karpūrikā, meeting *en route* with strange adventures, and lighting upon a city where a king lives with people who are automatons of wood: he has also flying machines, and one of these serves to bring the prince with Karpūrikā back to his home. Book VIII, again, has no essential connection with the tale; it is the narrative of how Sūryaprabha, king of Śākala, became emperor of the Vidyādharas after a great conflict with a rival, Śrutaśarman, which Śiva's intervention at last ended. The marvellous here is developed to an extent unprecedented in the rest of the work; old mythological figures, Buddhist beliefs, and popular legends are blended into a curious, sometimes fascinating, compound. In Book IX the hero acquires Alaṁkāravatī, who gives her name to the book, and takes part in a wonderful visit to a White Island, an episode closely parallel with the famous tale in the *Mahābhārata* of the visit of sages to such an island and of the wonderful god whom they found to be there adored, an episode which has often been adduced as proof of some knowledge of Christianity.[1] As in the epic, Nārada sings a hymn of praise which in Somadeva is uninteresting, but in Kṣemendra is expressed in prose with many compounds in his best Kāvya style. In X the hero acquires yet another wife, Śaktiyaśas, in XI, which is of only 115 verses, yet another, but the book is named after Velā, the heroine of the tale inserted in the main story. Book XII, Śaśāṅkavatī, tells of a marriage with a certain Lalitalocanā; in the course of his adventures with her he is told the story of Mṛgāṅkadatta and the heroine who gives the book its name; there is also included the *Vetālapañcaviṁśatikā* in full, so that the book is the longest of all. In XIII, Madiravatī, he recovers in some unexplained way his beloved. Only in Book XIV, Pañca, do we find the real essence of the tale, the rape of Madanamañcukā by Mānasavega, and the adventures of the prince to find her; in the course of these

[1] Cf. W. E. Clark, *J.A.O.S.*, xxxix, 209–42.

he is helped by Vegavatī, sister of his enemy, who possesses magic powers which she freely uses to aid him in his purpose, regains his beloved, weds five other Vidyādhara maidens, who had sworn to secure his love—whence the title of the book—and prepares to defeat his last rival, Mandaradeva. This he accomplishes in Book XV, attaining the Mahābhiṣeka, or imperial consecration. This is the real close of the work, but in Book XVI we have first an account of the death of Udayana and his wives by suicide and their ascent to heaven, and the tale of Suratamañjarī, daughter of a Vidyādhara, under the shape of a Mātaṅga in charge of elephants, and Avantivardhana. In Books XVII and XVIII we have legends of Padmāvatī, the wife of the Vidyādhara emperor, Muktāphalaketu, and of Viṣamaśīla, the latter giving the cycle of Vikramāditya legends. These are worked into the tale as having served to while away the time during the hero's search for his beloved.

It is plain that Books XII and XIII on the one hand, and the last two books on the other, are unsatisfactorily placed; all of them ought to be worked into the texture of the hero's adventures after the loss of his beloved. In effect we find this recognised in the order adopted in Kṣemendra; he agrees in Books I–V with his successor, but for the rest the order is: Śaūryaprabha, Madanamñcukā, Velā, Śaśāṅkavatī, Viṣamaśīla, Madiravatī, Padmāvatī, Pañca, Ratnaprabhā, Alaṁkāravatī, Śaktiyaśas, Mahābhiṣeka, Suratamañjarī. The books correspond generally save in the case of Velā; the decisive step is taken here of adding to it the episode of the rape of Madanamañcukā, so that the following books fall into effective order.

In addition to the main story, and frequently burying it, there are large numbers of interesting narratives of every kind. The task of deciding how far these belonged to the original of Guṇāḍhya is doubtless insoluble; it is plausible, however, to suppose that the *Bṛhatkathā* proper began with a Kathāmukha, which contained the episode of Suratamañjarī, and passed to the tale of Udayana, his marriage with Vāsavadattā, the Lāvāṇaka, the birth of Naravāhanadatta, the marriage with Madanamañcukā, his loss of her, and final winning of her after many adventures and new loves, terminating with his consecration as emperor.

The high age of the *Vetālapañcaviṁśatikā*, a prose recension of which is attributed to Śivadāsa, perhaps a Jain, is attested by the occurrence of the set of tales in both versions from Kashmir. They exist also as an independent collection,[1] twenty-five tales written in easy prose with quoted verses and verse fragments derived from the original. Its wide popularity is attested by the perplexing variations of the text.[2] The framework of the stories is simple; king Vikrama is bidden, for the purpose of a magic rite, to fetch from a cemetery a corpse hanging there on a tree, and this is to be done in absolute silence. A demon, however, which has entered into the corpse, narrates a tale to the king, as he bears along his horrid burden, and at the close puts a question arising from the tale to the king, who, naturally enough, falls into the trap and answers it, with the result that his task has to be done all over again. The tales are of varied interest, but all propose issues inviting casuistry. Thus we have the tale of the daughter of a Brahmin who has three suitors, so that her father was in a quandary as to how to bestow this pearl of beauty. A black snake solved the problem to all appearance by killing the damsel, and the father proceeds to burn her dead body. The three lovers go to the cemetery; one perishes with the body of his dear one; one builds a little hut there and abides in sorrow; one becomes a begging monk and sets out on his travels. In the course of them he enters a Brahmin's house to obtain a meal, and sees to his horror the mistress of the house cast into the fire the child which annoys her by crying. Indignant, he declines to break bread in such a house, but the Brahmin brings from an inner room a large book, reads aloud a magic formula, and the child is again in life. The lover sees his chance to revive his lost one; in the night he penetrates to the inner apartment and seizes the book. Returned to the cemetery he recalls to life the dead girl, and the youth who burned himself beside her revives. The old dispute now begins, and the vampire bids the king resolve it. This is too tempting an opportunity to exhibit his skill;

[1] Śivadāsa's recension is ed. by Uhle, Leipzig, 1881, with an anon. version; also from a MS. of A.D. 1487, Leipzig, 1914; a Jain one, of Jambhaladatta, is ed. Calcutta, 1873. See further N. M. Penzer, *Ocean of Story*, vi and vii; J. Hertel, *Streitberg Festgabe*, pp. 135 ff.

[2] The Hindī *Baitāl Pacīsī* rests ultimately on Śivadāsa's version.

Vikrama renders all his toil in vain by the sage pronouncement: 'He who has reanimated the maiden is her father, because he has given her life; he who died with her is her brother, because he is born along with her; her husband will be he who remained near her tomb.'

Of equally doubtful date is the popular collection of seventy tales of a parrot, *Śukasaptati*,[1] which the pleasing bird narrates in order to refrain its erring mistress from betraying her absent husband. The bird is willing to let his mistress adventure, but only if she has sufficient coolness and cleverness to get out of difficulties as did so and so. Inevitably the bait is successful; the lady must know the story and sacrifices a night to learn it, only to find next night the wise bird ready with another. Nor are the stories without others interwoven; in one the king is at dinner with his wife, when the naughty fishes on the table laugh at one of her remarks; the king is determined to know why, but the daughter of a minister warns him that if he persist he may rue his indiscretion, as did so and so; hence yet another story, until finally we have the laughter explained, not precisely in a manner to add to our admiration for the standard of royal morals. The work, indeed, insists on the ability of wives to deceive their husbands, and to exact from them apologies for very justly suspecting their conduct. Here, again, we have divergent versions, and the prose makes some pretensions to ornament. We find also some attempts at mannered description in the Jain version, especially, of the *Siṁhāsanadvātriṁśikā*,[2] a set of thirty-two tales told by the images which supported the throne of Vikramāditya. Like the *Śukasaptati* and the *Vetālapañcaviṁśatikā*, this text has found great favour in modern dialects.

The close relation between the tale and the more elaborate romance has already been seen. Daṇḍin shows the same spirit as Guṇāḍhya in the conception of his subject as the histories of princes reduced to vagabondage, meeting with

[1] *Textus simplicior*, ed. R. Schmidt, Leipzig, 1893; trs. Kiel, 1894; *ornatior*, ed. Munich, 1898; trs. Stuttgart, 1899. The date is dubious; a version is known to Hemacandra, *Yogaśāstra*, p. 444; Hertel, *Das Pañcatantra*, pp. 234 ff.

[2] For its four recensions see F. Edgerton, *Harvard Oriental Series*, xxvi, xxvii, 1926.

curious and not specially edifying adventures; he expressly makes Rājavāhana, a contemporary of Naravāhanadatta, and the episode of the chain, which binds him and turns into a beautiful maiden seems a literal application of a metaphorical turn in the *Bṛhatkathā* preserved to us by Budhasvāmin. The influence is obvious also in the case of the *Yaśastilaka*, where the hero also becomes an emperor, and more faintly in the *Tilakamañjarī*. From Abhinanda of Kashmir in the ninth century[1] we have an epitome of the *Kādambarī*, the *Kādambarīkathāsara*, and the Jain literature is full of Kathās of varied kind and date, as, for instance, in Hemacandra's *Pariśiṣṭaparvan*.

In the Buddhist literature we have not merely such works as the *Divyāvadāna*[2] and the *Avadānaśataka*,[3] but also the *Jātakamālā*[4] of Ārya Śūra, perhaps in the fourth century A.D., which is of interest among other things for both form and style. It is written in prose with many interspersed verses, in part gnomic, in part narrative, and both show every sign of the Kāvya style.[5] We have here, as in Aśvaghoṣa, the determination to apply to Buddhism the processes of the higher literature, and we may judge from the *Jātakamālā* the character of the style of the *Sūtrālaṁkāra*, which in itself is only too vaguely presented through the medium of the translation.[6]

[1] Thomas, *Kavīndravacanasamuccaya*, p. 20.
[2] Ed. E. B. Cowell and R. A. Neil, Cambridge, 1886.
[3] Ed. J. S. Speyer, Petrograd, 1902–9; trs. L. Feer, Paris, 1891.
[4] Ed. H. Kern, Boston, 1891; trs. J. S. Speyer, London, 1895.
[5] Compare the Campū style, above, chap. vi.
[6] This impression is confirmed by the fragments transcribed by Lüders, according to which the title of the work is *Kalpanāmaṇḍitikā*. Cf. p. 25.

VIII

THE DIDACTIC FABLE

THE closeness in which the Indians lived with nature rendered it inevitable that the didactic fable should form at an early date a normal feature of village life, and that it should be reflected in literature. The *Ṛgveda*[1] already compares the croaking of the frogs at the beginning of the rains to the Brahmins busy at the offering, and the *Chāndogya Upaniṣad*[2] knows a mysterious Udgītha of the dogs which may be a parable, or a record of ascetics who imitated the life of dogs in a crazy effort thus to attain salvation, but in any case shows realistically how ready was Indian thought to ascribe to animals like thoughts and deeds to men, a tendency accentuated by the rising belief in transmigration involving frequent animal rebirths. In the epic[3] we find fables used to illustrate policy; Vidura bids Dhṛtarāṣṭra not to persecute the Pāṇḍavas lest he kill the bird that gave gold. We learn also of the cat whose piety deceived the mice into trusting him, enabling him to eat them all, and the advice is given to treat the Pāṇḍavas as the clever jackal did his friends, the tiger, mouse, ichneumon, and wolf, when, having won a prize by their aid, he cheated them of any share in the booty. The vagueness of the date of the epic is redeemed by the monumental evidence of Buddhist *Jātakas* at Bharhut, which establishes the beast fable as current in the second century B.C., at which date we have also, as has been seen,[4] hints in the *Mahābhāṣya*. In Buddhism, however, the fable was given a definite religious significance, by being employed in connection with the doctrine of transmigration to illustrate the essential virtues of Buddhism, through the identification

[1] vii, 103. [2] i, 12.
[3] Winternitz, *Gesch. d. ind. Litt.*, i, 348–50.
[4] Above, p. 14.

of personages of the tales with the Buddha and others of his *entourage*.

Equally characteristic and important was the employment given to the fable in Sanskrit literature. The artless tale must often in its inception have been devoid of moral or other purpose, beyond the giving of pleasure and the passing of time. In the new form in which it has influenced so greatly Indian and Western literature, the didactic motive which is latent is deliberately and expressly developed, and stories are now grouped in connected series within a framework in order definitely to give precepts, a creation which, of course, takes us away from folk literature, and reveals the intellectual subtlety and skill of the Brahmins. Further, this skill was not exercised for the benefit of the priestly class solely or primarily. The conception of the composition was developed for the service of the Court, that the minds of princes should be imbued in the most pleasant way with the principles of statecraft policy and practical life generally, all the topics, in fact, which are summed up in the term Arthaśāstra or Nītiśāstra, for the two are closely connected. This fact is important, for it accounts for the fact, at first sight curious, that the tales often illustrate rather dubious morals, and cannot by any effort of the imagination be said to present a creditable set of ideals. This difficulty disappears, when we realise that the aim was not to illustrate the Brahmanical moral code, but to give useful advice for political and practical life. We must not, however, exaggerate this aspect or conceive the stories as each intended to show some clever trick; Indian political life was not so corrupt as to reduce statecraft to mere Machiavellian devices, and there is much sound sense, which usually means sound morality, in the collection.

The form of the work is characteristic of the progress of classical Sanskrit literature.[1] There can be no doubt that the earliest text, whence the various forms of the *Pañcatantra* are derived, deliberately aimed at literary merit. Sanskrit, we know from the epigraphical records, began to reassert itself in the latter part of the second century A.D. as the

[1] A reconstruction of the *Pañcatantra* is attempted by F. Edgerton, New Haven, 1924.

language of the Court, and the princes were doubtless in need of text-books, which would at one and the same time instruct them in the language of diplomacy and public affairs—largely in the hands of Sanskrit-speaking Brahmins—and afford them valuable lessons in policy. Hence we can understand the appearance of a proto-*Pañcatantra* in which the Kāvya style was applied, doubtless in a simple form, to the subject matter of policy. We do not know the title of this lost work, nor its author, though probably it was already cast in the form of instruction given by the octogenarian, Viṣṇuśarman, to the sons, ignorant of Arthaśāstra, of the king Amaraśakti of Mihilāropya, presumably a mythical prince. It may have been called *Pañcatantra* or *Tantrākhyāyika*; in either case Tantra may have denoted politics as art or science, though it is conceivable that it meant no more than book. The oldest form of this proto-*Pañcatantra* preserved to us is probably a Kashmir version, the *Tantrākhyāyika*,[1] which may denote stories to illustrate politics, and at any rate indicates the connection of the new genre with the Ākhyāyikā.

The date of the original text is unluckily quite uncertain in the absence of any very distinctive characteristic. It alludes, however, to Cāṇakya, which immediately places it after 300 B.C., and it undoubtedly shows signs of knowing some of the substance of the work which passes as the *Kauṭilīya Arthaśāstra*. But this carries us no further, for there is no proof either that it followed the *Arthaśāstra* as we have it, or of the real date of that text, which is probably to be placed some centuries A.D.[2] A lower limit is definitely given by the fact that in substance and even in form, the major part of the text is doubtless anterior to A.D. 570, the date of the Syriac version of the Pahlavi translation of the original, at least in all essentials.[3] More precise evidence is suggested by the occurrence of the

[1] Ed. by J. Hertel, 1910, and trs. 1909; see also *Das Pañcatantra* (1914), pp. 8 ff.

[2] Keith, *J.R.A.S.*, 1915, pp. 130–37; 1920, p. 628; Jolly, *Z.D.M.G.*, lxviii, 355 ff.; lxix, 369 ff.; *Zeitschrift für vergl. Rechtswissenschaft*, xxxvii, 329; Winternitz, *Gesch. d. ind. Litt.*, iii, 518; O. Stein, *Megasthenes und Kauṭilya* (1921).

[3] That there was a Prākrit original is disproved in *Das Pañcatantra*, p. 430, n. 1.

term, Dīnāra, which is, of course, a borrowing from denarius, but through a form in which the pronunciation of the *e* had become *ī*. Unluckily the precise date when this took place is uncertain, and we cannot certainly[1] conclude thence that the work must be placed as late as A.D. 300, though on general grounds there is no reason to demand an earlier date. Further, it seems probable that the text was the outcome of the Brahmanical revival of the Gupta epoch. Dr. Hertel, indeed, takes the view that it was a product of Kashmir, which Professor Franke made out to be the home of classical Sanskrit,[2] but for either suggestion there is no tolerable evidence. The fact that the *Tantrākhyāyika* is preserved there is worthless as proof, and the fact, if it were established, that neither the tiger nor the elephant plays a part in the original *Pañcatantra*, while, on the other hand, the camel, which is not an all-Indian beast, was known, would be quite insufficient in the case of a work of so late a date to suggest original production in Kashmir. At the date assumed for production, the elephant and the tiger must have been known to everyone there, and equally the camel must have been familiar to the learned and unlearned public of many parts of India. On the other hand, we may readily believe that the author was neither a Buddhist nor a Jain, but a Brahmin, and perhaps more definitely a Vaiṣṇava, though the syncretism and pantheism of Brahmanism render dogmatism on such a point dangerous.

The *Tantrākhyāyika* is preserved, like so many other texts, in slightly differing forms, each one with some interpolation. In its original text it consisted of five books, each with a main story and tales interwoven. Book I deals with the separation of friends, telling with the help of seventeen tales how two jackals, Karaṭaka and Damanaka, succeeded in estranging the lion and the bull who were once inseparable. Book II, with five tales, expounds the winning of friends by the illustration of the union effected between the dove, mouse, crow, tortoise and deer through mutual helpfulness. Book III, with eleven tales, tells of the war of the hereditary foes, the crows and the owls, whose enmity is alluded to in the *Mahābhāṣya*. Books IV and V have each but two tales; they

[1] Keith, *J.R.A.S.*, 1915, p. 504 f.

[2] *Pāli und Sanskrit* (1902). Contrast Lüders, *Bruchstücke buddh. Dramen*, p. 63, n. 5.

discourse of the loss of one's gettings and the fruit of rashness. To these may be added four further tales, which appear to Dr. Hertel unoriginal. The construction is not normally complex; the tales usually are simply inserted in the framework of the story, being told to illustrate some maxim which is laid down in the main narrative, and causes a digression. But here and there the structure is more elaborate; thus in Book I the tale of the strand bird and the sea rises naturally out of the main narrative, but into it are interpolated, first, the narrative of the two geese and the tortoise, and then later that of the three fishes. More complex still is the case of tale one of Book II, for in it is inserted the famous story of hulled grain for hulled grain, and in the latter again the anecdote of the over-greedy jackal, but this degree of complication is not repeated.

Of the attraction and interest of the collection no doubt has ever existed. None can mistake the delicate sense of humour of the author, whose name unhappily is lost to us; his animals charm us with the quaint propriety of the sentiments and speeches ascribed to them; the stories have the same appeal to us as the animals in Kipling's *Jungle Book*, reminding us of the common humanity which, after all, underlies the enormous superficial differences between the races of men. Admirable is the tale of the lion and the hare, which, marked out as the daily offering to induce the lion to abstain from promiscuous murder, arrives late to the place of sacrifice, and excuses itself by the intervention of another lion. The deluded lord of the forest decides first to slay this rival and then enjoy his meal; but his fate is at hand, for he is shown his imaged presentment in a well, and, leaping against his foe, perishes by a deserved doom. A hare, again, is the hero of a story in which, by clever use of the reflection in the water of the moon, whose visage bears a harelike mark, it gets rid of an elephant which had become a nuisance to all concerned. A Brahmin's gullibility is related in the tale of how three rogues cheated him out of the goat he was carrying for a sacrificial victim, by assuring him in turn that it was an unclean animal, a dog, thus conquering his natural trust of his own vision. If this story has no very elevated moral, it is compensated for by the legend of king Śibi, famous in the literature, who sacrificed his own flesh to satisfy a hungry hawk, from which he protected a dove fleeing to him for refuge; the gods Dharma and Indra revealed themselves and commend his self-sacrifice. The Buddhist flavour of the tale and the scorn of Brahmins sometimes shown remind us of the varied sources whence the writer derived the material which he formed into shape. Another note is struck in the narrative of the tiny mouse, which fell from a hawk's mouth into the hand of a seer, who tenderly reared it, having changed it into a maiden. In due course he resolved on a marriage for her, but an equal must be found; the sun, offered the prize, modestly declines, because the clouds are mightier than he, since they can obscure his light; but the clouds also have a master, the wind, which drives them hither and thither. The wind is appealed to, but the mountains defy his every blast; they, too, admit one superior, for the mice ever gnaw holes in them. The seer rightly, therefore, bestows the hand of the damsel on a mouse and restores to her the shape necessary to enter her spouse's abode. Famous in its history is the legend of the onion thief,[1] who, captured in the act, is offered the choice of three penalties—the paying of a hundred rupees, the infliction of a hundred lashes, or the eating of a hundred onions. He chooses the last, but seven or eight of them bring streams of tears to his eyes and he hastily tries the lashing instead. This also is too much, and he falls back on paying the fine, thus earning popular contempt and the pain of his experiences. In the last book we have the famous and pathetic tale of the Brahmin, who slew in hasty folly the faithful ichneumon, which had slain the serpent that attacked the child left in his care. It is noteworthy that the narrative is illustrated by the tale of the Brahmin who indulged in dreams of the prosperity to be made out of skilful employment of the groats he had begged; the upshot would be the gaining of a wife, who however, would require correction for neglect of the infant which would crown their union, but the beautiful dream comes to an end by the upsetting of the pot of groats over the day-dreamer, a just rebuke for his assertion even in a dream of the right of marital correction. In these tales again we see reflected the popular source of some of the compilations.

[1] Cf. Zachariae, *Vienna Or. Journ.*, xxvi, 425 ff.

The style of the work is simple and elegant; it is in prose as regards the narrative, but this is interspersed by verses of gnomic character, sometimes in considerable numbers; thus in the tale of Somilaka (II, 4) a divine being addresses five stanzas to the weaver asserting the doctrine of fate, while Somilaka replies in the same number, and there are several even longer sets. Verses also form the means of introducing the tales within the framework, as a stanza recited containing a reference to some story affords the motive for the question which elicits a new tale. This type of composition we find already foreshadowed in the *Aitareya Brāhmaṇa*[1] and its naturalness is obvious. The summing up of moral or political maxims in verse, while the mere narrative moves in prose, produces at once an artistic and a plausible result. The sources of the verses are various; most of them come doubtless from the vast body of maxims which were in circulation, and of which many are enshrined in the *Mahābhārata* or in the Pāli *Jātakas*.[2] The merit of the author lies, therefore, not in composing them, but in the selection of appropriate stanzas and their skilful introduction into the text, and his merits in this regard are obvious. Thus in a stanza found in a variant form in Bhartṛhari the power of action to bear fruit is asserted:

Beauty bears no fruit, nor virtue, nor valour; nor yet knowledge, nor laborious service. But, as trees bear fruit, so the accumulation of merit of ancient deeds in due season brings fruition to man.

It is indeed difficult to exaggerate the value added to the text by the citation of graceful verses, of general human interest, balancing the primary absorption in the affairs of the beasts of the fables:

Firm in purpose he will enter fire; easy for him to leap over the vast ocean. Nothing indeed do I know that may not easily be accomplished by a man of abiding resolution, who will not brook defeat.

Better the man of action than the man of words alone, for it is human action that brings ambrosia or poison, according as the actor is good or bad.

The poor man feels shame; overcome by shame he loses pride; lacking pride he is despised; despised he becomes depressed; depres-

[1] Cf. Keith, *Rigveda Brāhmaṇas*, pp. 63 ff.; above, pp. 83, 95.
[2] Hertel, trs., i, 146 f.

sion leads to sorrow; sorrow dims the intelligence; ruin awaits the fool; ah! poverty is the root of all misfortune.

Better to thrust one's hands into an angry serpent's mouth, better to drink poison and sleep in Yama's halls, better to cast oneself from a hill top and be dashed into a hundred fragments than to find pleasure in wealth won by rogues.

Loves that last for life, anger that is swiftly past, easy partings, these are alien to the magnanimous.

The purpose of the book, instruction for young princes, necessitates the adoption of a form of prose which is normally easy to comprehend; the compounds are usually moderate in length and without complication, and, though the use of participles—passive and active—in narration is frequent, there are many finite verbs, imperfect, perfect, and aorist, all occurring indiscriminately as narrative tenses. Rare words or grammatical obscurities are few, especially when the defective condition of the manuscript evidence is borne in mind. Indeed, rarely in Sanskrit literature is the style more admirably adapted to the subject matter and the purpose of the work.[1] None of the later versions can be said artistically to stand higher than the *Tantrākhyāyika*.

That the *Tantrākhyāyika* not only is superior to the later versions, but represents the original more faithfully than they, is shown by the closeness of the correspondence between it and the Pahlavi version, which, considering that that version was only a translation and is known to us through a further translation, must be regarded as remarkable. There were certain changes made and a few omissions, but we need not place the original *Pañcatantra* at any great distance of time from the *Tantrākhyāyika*.

In the view of Dr. Hertel, which is still unproved,[2] all other versions known of the proto-*Pañcatantra*, may be derived from a Kashmir codex, now lost. From it ultimately came a version of the *Pañcatantra*, which was interpolated, with matter intervening between the five books, in the *Bṛhatkathā* of Guṇāḍhya in a revised text of that work, which existed in the north-west before the eleventh century A.D., when it

[1] Interesting as precursors of the later Kāvya style are the occasional aggregation of epithets, and the use of rhythmic prose (e.g. pp. 8, 69 and 118 of *MS.A.*).

[2] Cf. F. Edgerton, *Am. Journ. Phil.*, xxxvi, 253 ff., and his later views in his reconstruction of the *Pañcatantra* (1924).

formed the basis of the summaries of the *Bṛhatkathā* made in Sanskrit, first by Kṣemendra and then by Somadeva. Kṣemendra, it is clear, used also a version of the *Tantrākhyāyika*, so that his work does not accurately represent the revised *Bṛhatkathā*. From the same ultimate source[1] an epitome was made, containing all the stories and most of the verses; the date of this epitome was probably after Kālidāsa, as a verse (ii, 55) from the *Kumārasambhava* is used. This epitome is represented, with considerable precision by the *Southern Pañcatantra*.[2] Little is added, including, however, one whole story of the cowherdess and her lover (I, 12), but the condensation of the narrative, which in the original was not prolix, has led to difficulty here and there in understanding details. The lower limit of date of the *Southern Pañcatantra* cannot be determined. This epitome was recast by some unknown hand, the order of Books I and II being inverted, and this recast is preserved for us in two forms, the Nepalese *Pañcatantra* and the *Hitopadeśa*. The former as preserved gives the verses only of the recast, with certain omissions—probably because the copyist mistook them for prose—and one piece of prose, clearly mistaken for verse.

The *Hitopadeśa*,[3] on the other hand, represents a deliberate attempt to reconstruct the *Pañcatantra* by the introduction of new matter. It is indeed based on the recast of the epitome which is seen in the *Southern Pañcatantra*, but the author has used another collection of fables, as he expressly indicates in his preface, giving seventeen new stories, and has added many verses from the *Kāmandaki Nītiśāstra* in illustration of his theme. Not only has he preserved the transposition of Books I and II as in the recast evidenced by the Nepalese version, but he has omitted Book IV. Book III he has divided into two, and has included between the two new books the contents of the original Book V and part of Book I, which in the original is of very marked disparity to the rest as regards

[1] An independent source is more probable.

[2] See J. Hertel, *Das Pañcatantra* (1914), pp. 35 ff.; ed. Leipzig, 1906. Possibly it is later than Bhāravi (ii, 30).

[3] Ed. P. Peterson, Bombay, 1887. It dates after Māgha, and before A.D. 1373. It recognises the Tantric cult of Gaurī, popular in Bengal, and it mentions Sunday as *bhaṭṭārakavara*, suggesting a date not before A.D. 900.

the number of the stories. The result is that the books are much more in agreement as regards number of stories and length. The author of the *Hitopadeśa* has left us his name. He was Nārāyaṇa, and his patron a certain Dhavalacandra, whose home may have been in Bengal where the *Hitopadeśa* is in special favour. It undoubtedly deserves its vogue.

An expansion as opposed to a reduction of the original is seen in the version of the *Pañcatantra* which is widely current in India, the so-called *textus simplicior.*[1] In the north-west and in central India the *Pañcākhyānaka*, as it is called in an old manuscript, has superseded the original entirely. The author may have been a Jain; the evidence is presumptive, not conclusive. He took many liberties with the text; like the author of the *Hitopadeśa*, he aimed at equalising the contents of the books; for this purpose he added several tales to the short Book V, and increased Book IV by taking some stories from Book III. Moreover, he added several other stories, kept most of the verses of the original, but added many more, and beyond all he freely re-wrote the prose, ignoring the original. The result, it must be admitted, is decidedly satisfactory, but the popularity of the work has played havoc with the preservation of the text, the manuscripts differing indefinitely, nor is it possible to trace the precise sources of the alterations made. As a verse of Rudra Bhaṭṭa[2] is cited, it is probable that the work is not earlier than the eleventh century. In A.D. 1199 it was made use of by a Jain Pūrṇabhadra, in producing a new version,[3] the so-called *textus ornatior.* He takes Book V largely from the *textus simplicior*, and allows himself to be influenced by it throughout. But he knew also a version of the *Tantrākhyāyika*, whence he adopted the correct order of stories in Book III. His language is marked by occasional Prākritisms and influences of his vernacular, Gujarātī, are discernible. His version and that of the *textus simplicior* have greatly

[1] Cf. Bühler and Kielhorn's ed., *Bombay Sanskrit Series*, Nos. 1, 3 and 4.

[2] Not Rudraṭa as stated by Hertel, *Das Pañcatantra*, p. 72, and repeatedly later. Rudra is cited by Hemacandra (Hari Chand, *Kālidāsa*, p. 112).

[3] Ed. *Harvard Oriental Series*, xii (1912).

influenced the many mixed versions in Sanskrit and in vernaculars which are known in India.

To the Western world the *Pañcatantra* was introduced by the enterprise of the physician Barzōe,[1] or Barzuyeh, who under the patronage of Chosrau Anosharwān (A.D. 531–79) translated, under the title Karaṭaka and Damanaka, a version of the *Pañcatantra* into Pahlavi. The text used must have closely represented the same original as the *Tantrākhyāyika*, when allowance is made for the obvious demerits of the translator, who found the difficult passages, and specially the verses, beyond his capacity. This version is lost, but is known to us from two primary sources, a translation into Old Syriac made in A.D. 570 by one Būd, preserved in a single manuscript, and an Arabic rendering, made about A.D. 750, by Abdallah ibn al Muqaffa' under the style *Kalīlah wa Dimnah*. From this rendering are derived the other versions of the West and East. In 1251 an Old Spanish rendering was made, and considerably before that date (*c.* A.D. 1100) a rendering in Hebrew by Rabbi Joel. This was turned into Latin by John of Capua, a Jew convert to Christianity, between 1263 and 1278, and this was printed in 1480, under the title of *Directorium vitæ humanæ*. From it came the German rendering, *Das buch der byspel der alten wysen*, by Anthonius von Pforr, which was printed in that or the following year and became very popular. From the Latin also was taken the Italian version of A. F. Doni, printed in two parts at Venice in 1552; the first of these was rendered by Sir Thomas North, and printed at London in 1570. The most important use made of these fables was that of La Fontaine, whose second edition (1678) of the Fables is largely based as regards the new matter added (vii–xi) on the fables of Pilpay, which is usually held to be the corrupted form through the Arabic of Vidyāpati, a complimentary style not originally a proper name. Direct from the Arabic came also the Greek version of about 1080, the later Syriac of the tenth or eleventh century, and the Persian of Naṣrallāh in the twelfth century, whence comes the much better known Anwāri Suhailī dated 1494.

[1] Doubt has recently been cast on the existence of Barzōe, but it is clear that there was a Pahlavi version, and that alone is of importance.

IX

LYRIC AND GNOMIC VERSE

KĀLIDĀSA's work evoked many lyrics, but nothing ever emerged to rival successfully the *Meghadūta*. Tradition of no value, that of the nine gems of Vikramāditya's Court, would make contemporary with him the author of the *Ghaṭakarpara*, potsherd, which bears its author's name, and is marked by the use of Yamakas, of which it boasts. It is probable that it owes its fame and preservation not to its small intrinsic merit, but to the fact that its author was a pioneer in the useless art of constructing a poem with these repetitions of sounds. To Kālidāsa himself is attributed the *Śṛṅgāratilaka*,[1] which in twenty-three stanzas, one more than the *Ghaṭakarpara*, works out effectively some quaint analogies of love. A maiden is a hunter, her bow the bow he bends, her glances his arrows, and the heart the deer he slays. A maiden again has a heart of stone, though her features and her limbs are tender as flowers. Doubtless the ascription is without value, and emphatically may this be said of the wretched taste, which attributes to him so artificial and worthless a poem as the *Rākṣasakāvya*, whose one merit is that it gives commentators an opportunity of showing their erudition.

Probably contemporaneous with, or a little earlier than, Kālidāsa were those poets whose work went to constitute the collection of some 700 stanzas passing under the name of Hāla or Sātavāhana,[2] who is known to Bāṇa in the *Harṣacarita*. Written in artificial and carefully studied language, the Māhārāṣṭrī Prākrit, and metre, they show, none the less, a measure of naturalness which is doubtless

[1] Regarded as genuine by Hillebrandt, *Kālidāsa*, p. 156, n. 81.

[2] Ed. and trs., A. Weber, Leipzig, 1881; ed. *Kāvyamālā*, No. 21. A later anthology is the *Vajjālagga* of Jayavallabha, before A.D. 1300; J. Laber, *Ueber das Vajjâlaggam* (1913); it is being ed. in the *Bibl. Ind.*

the reflex of the matter of fact spirit of the Marāṭha people. Among much that is sensual or licentious, trivial or hackneyed we find many effective expressions of the sentiment of love:

Short, say they, are the nights in summer; but, ah! they are long for me, far from my beloved. For half the year the days grow longer, for the other half the nights. How different the year of separation! Then the days and the nights grow equally long.

The true accent of the tenderness of a loving maiden is revealed in:

Well do I know that he has wronged me, that his word is false. Yet, when he begs my pardon, it is I who feel at fault.

Sly humour is not wanting. Yaśodā may say that Kṛṣṇa is but a child, but the maidens of the village smile involuntarily as they look at the alleged infant. Pretty is the picture of the angry and offended wife at whose feet the false husband falls in penitence. The pathetic effect is ruined by their little boy, who seizes the opportunity to climb on papa's back so that the justly incensed matron can only laugh. The thirsty traveller feasts his eyes on the maiden who draws water for him, and, to prolong the feast, lets the water escape through his fingers, while she, with equal desire, lessens the stream of water which she directs into his hands. The beauty of the garland-maker's arms, as she plys her trade, attracts the lover who has no intention of purchasing her wares. The maiden, who guards the field of rice, is so fair that she has no rest from the passers-by, who insist on asking her the way, however well they know it. The moon is a white flamingo sailing in silver beauty upon the pure lake of the heaven at night, and the stars that glitter are the lotuses of the lake. 'Though my gaze go to the furthest bound,' a lover says, 'yet dost thou stand before me; the heaven and the beauty of the stars are a picture of thee.' Here and there a more dubious note is struck: 'The night is very dark; my husband is from home; the house is empty; pray come to guard me from robbers.'

So interesting a collection naturally found at last an imitator in Sanskrit. One of the Court poets of Lakṣmaṇasena of Bengal in the latter part of the twelfth century, Govardhana, owes to it the inspiration for his *Āryāsapta-*

śatī[1] in which he essays the difficult task of composing himself, in lieu of merely collecting, seven hundred stanzas, prevailingly erotic, without inner connection, and arranged merely by the artificial device of alphabetical order. The work falls into sections, named Vrajyās, as in Sādhāraṇadeva's recension of the *Saptaśataka* of Hāla and in Jayavallabha's *Vajjālagga*; the first contains seventy-three stanzas beginning with the letter *a*, not in strict alphabetical order, and the last has three beginning in *kṣ*. The influence of the late doctrine, which makes suggestion the vital element in poetry, is strongly present; often an erotic sense is indirectly expressed, as in the *Anyoktimuktālatā* of Śambhu (*c.* A.D. 1100), or the *Anyoktiśataka* of Vīreśvara of unknown date. In poetic value the work is indubitably inferior to Hāla's, despite the superior beauty of Sanskrit as a language.

In Sanskrit the highest distinction, as the poet who can depict the various phases of love, desire and attainment, estrangement and reconciliation, joy and sorrow, must be awarded to Amaru or Amarūka,[2] whose name is as strange as his date is doubtful. He figures as one of the gems of the Court of Vikramāditya, but it is impossible to suppose that he was really a contemporary of Kālidāsa. We definitely know that he dates before Ānandavardhana, and that he cannot be later, therefore, than about A.D. 800. The suggestion that his verses serve the prosaic, if useful, purpose of illustrating types of heroines, as in the case of Rudra Bhaṭṭa's *Śṛṅgāratilaka*,[3] may safely be discarded. The aim to be attained is the production in the reader of some definite phase of emotion, and this is to be achieved by a solitary stanza, a task of no small difficulty. It is very possible that the *Śataka* from the first contained work collected, not written, by the author, but of this clear proof is difficult, and the exact extent of the collection is obscured by the variations of recension. But the skill of the poet or poets is indubitable; thus of the newly-wedded wife we have a graceful and lively picture:

When her husband touches her garment, she bends her head in shyness; when he seeks a long embrace, unnoticed she moves away

[1] Ed. *Kāvyamālā*, No. 1. For the date cf. *Ind. Ant.*, li, 145 ff., and Chintaharan Chakravarti, *Indian Historical Quarterly*, iii, 186 ff.
[2] R. Simon, *Amarūśataka in seinen Recensionen dargestellt* (1893).
[3] Ed. Pischel, Kiel, 1886.

her limbs; when her eye falls on her laughing friends she cannot address them; at the first jest her heart is overwhelmed with bashfulness.

At the first wrong done her by her husband the young wife cannot, without her friend's aid, think of a witty rebuke to address to him, nor show her emotion by the movement of her limbs; wildly her eyes roll, while her clear tears pour down her pure cheeks and her waving hair is tossed in confusion as she weeps.

Seeing their chamber empty, the young wife slowly rose from her couch, and gazed long on the face of her husband who feigned sleep; then fearlessly she kissed him until she saw him thrilled by her touch, when she bent her head in shame, only to be given a long and loving kiss as he laughed at her distress.

'Why did I not, in my folly, cling to the neck of my heart's beloved? Why, when he kissed me, did I move away my face? Why did I not gaze upon him? Why did I not speak to him?' Thus speaks, in remorse at her coldness when a new-made bride, the tender lady, who now knows the savour of the love that rages within her.

'Why so thin thy limbs? Why dost thou tremble? And why, beloved, so pale thy cheek?' When the lord of her life thus questions her, the slender lady replies, 'It is but my nature,' as she moves away and lets fall elsewhere, with a sigh, the burden of tears which weigh down her eyelashes.

Most graceful and true to life is the picture of the angry maiden who yet loves dearly:

'Though my heart burst and Love at his pleasure emaciate my frame, yet, my dear friend, I will have no more of my fickle lover,' thus hotly in her high anger spoke the gazelle-eyed one, but anxiously did she gaze on the path by which her beloved would come.

The picture of love normally treats it as fulfilled, or assured of fulfilment; it is seldom that a note of despair is struck, though warnings against carrying anger or hauteur too far are given, and even the final loss of love is faced:

'Why, angry one, dost cry and ever brush away with thy fingertips the flood of thy tears? Thou wilt weep more bitterly still, for thy beloved will care no more to soothe thee, wearied of the pride that hath soared too high at the bidding of treacherous friends.'

'The bond of love is broken, departed the honour of his affection, lost his friendship, and my loved one goeth before me as a stranger; when I see this and think of the days that are over, I know not, dear friend, why my heart doth not break in a hundred pieces.'

Normally, however, there is no more than the grief of temporary parting; the Indian poet does not describe the bitterness of love lost on one who does not return it, or on one whom fate takes irrevocably away. But he excels in pictures of the sorrows of temporary separation of husband and wife, when the former as often must go on journey. Sometimes the tears of the wife forbid departure at all, but if he must go, then her feelings are forcibly described:

> The wife of the traveller gazes on the way by which her husband must come, so far as the eye can reach, until, as night falls, and darkness comes on, confusing the paths, discouraged and sorrowful, she takes one step to return to her home, but swiftly turns again her head to gaze, lest even at that very moment he may have come back.

Wider in their range and even more famous are the three *Śatakas*, which treat of love (*śṛṅgāra*), of resignation (*vairāgya*), and of conduct or policy (*nīti*). There is no adequate ground to doubt that the centuries were collected by the author of the *Vākyapadiya*, whose death took place, according to the Chinese pilgrim, I-Tsing, about A.D. 650, and whose Buddhist associations are attested independently by Indian evidence.[1] The *Vākyapadiya*[2] contains a good deal that is interesting on the philosophy of speech, and there is nothing in it inconsistent with the taste that would gather the centuries or compose part of the verses. Bhartṛhari, I-Tsing tells us, was one of those who took and broke lightly, as the lax rules of Buddhism permit, monastic vows, wavering no less than seven times between the comparative charms of the monastery and the world, though this may be no more than an early legend, based on the striking contrast of his century of love and his century of resignation. The love stanzas contain much that is affecting and beautiful, including the image of the love god as a fisher who casts women as his bait on the ocean of the world, catches men attracted by the lure of red lips, and bakes them on the fire of love. Or the god is conceived as the robber who dwells in the dread forest of women's beauty, in which the unwary is forbidden to set foot. Love is all-conquering, subduing even the learned who affect to scorn his sway; the world is dark without the light of the eyes of the beloved. But again, love is for youth; in old age wisdom rejects it and turns to resignation. This

[1] Pathak, *J.B.R.A.S.*, xviii, 341–49. The Śatakas are ed. Bombay, 1905; trs. B. H. Wortham, London, 1886.

[2] Ed. Benares, 1884–1907.

sentiment is expressed with force and beauty in many forms; pleasure is vain, nothing is real, self-sacrifice alone counts:

> The things of sense will leave us early or late, however long they may remain with us, and, since we must part from them, why not let them go with good-will? When it is they that flee us, they leave unspeakable sorrow behind; but, when we lay them aside we gain internal peace and bliss ineffable.
>
> Those that brought us up are long departed; those that grew old along with us are no more than a memory. We that remain are threatened at every moment by the same fate, broken like the trees on a sandbank.
>
> To man is allotted a span of a hundred years; half of that passes in sleep; of the other half one half is spent in childhood and old age; the rest is passed in service with illness, separation, and pain as companions. How can mortals find joy in life that is like the bubbles on the waves of the sea?

The same sentiments are re-echoed in the powerful *Mohamudgara*, attributed, with many other hymns of no mean merit, to Śaṅkara, though doubtless without warrant, and in the *Śāntiśataka* of the poet Śilhaṇa:[1] the latter is doubtless inferior in poetic power to Bhartṛhari, his tone is more sombre, but he shows also deeper feeling than his predecessor, and his Buddhist inspiration is more pronounced:

> A low fellow insults me; I shut myself up in the refuge of my patience, and happiness is mine for the moment. But now sorrow comes instead at the thought that I have caused that poor wretch to commit so grave a sin.
>
> Nothing here below, nothing elsewhere; wherever I go, nothing on every side; understood aright the whole universe is nothing; outside the self-consciousness of the individual there is nothing at all.

Perhaps older contemporaries of Bhartṛhari were Mayūra, father-in-law of Bāṇa and author of a *Sūryaśataka*,[2] a hundred stanzas in praise of the sun, which is a work of no inconsiderable merit, and Mātaṅga Divākara, of whom some stanzas are preserved. Of purely erotic type is the *Caurapañcāśikā*,

[1] Ed. K. Schönfeld, Leipzig, 1910; cf. Keith, *J.R.A.S.*, 1911, pp. 257 ff. That Bilhaṇa is the author may safely be negatived on grounds of style. The author is a Vaiṣṇava, and this fact explains some of his variations from Bhartṛhari.

[2] Ed. and trs., G. P. Quackenbos, New York, 1917, along with Bāṇa's *Caṇḍīśataka*, a praise of Durgā.

which is almost certainly[1] by Bilhaṇa, author of the *Vikramāṅkadevacarita*. There is, of course, no truth in the picturesque tradition which alleges that the poet contracted a secret union with a king's daughter, was captured and condemned to die, but won the heart of the sovereign by the touching verses, uttered as he was led to execution, in which he recalls the joys of the love that had been. It is highly probable that there is no personal experience at all in the lines, whose warmth of feeling undoubtedly degenerates into licence.

Of infinitely greater importance is the *Gītagovinda*[2] of Jayadeva, one of the Court poets of Lakṣmaṇasena of Bengal (*c.* A.D. 1180–1200), a contemporary of Govardhana, Dhoyī Śrutadhara Kavirāja,[3] Śaraṇa, and Umāpatidhara, who with him make up the five jewels in whose possession the Court of his patron vied with the nine of Vikramāditya, though with better historical warrant. The piece has been called a lyric drama, but, though it is doubtless based on the popular Kṛṣṇa festival celebrated in the Yātrā of Bengal,[4] it has no dramatic qualities proper; the songs, which are its essence, are not intended to be taken as statement and answer. It is idle to seek for the divisions of action appropriate to the true drama; instead the poet divides his work into twelve cantos, and twenty-four sections, composed in varied metres to be sung in sets of eight stanzas to different tunes. The songs are placed in the mouths of Kṛṣṇa, his beloved Rādhā, and a friend of the latter; they are introduced by verses setting out the situation which gives them birth, and they are followed by prayers addressed to Kṛṣṇa. This is something very different from the popular Yātrā; it is the creation of great poetic talent, which well deserves the honour paid to it by the use of the poem at festivals in honour of Kṛṣṇa, where the parts are sung to

[1] Bühler, *Kaśmīr Report*, p. 48 f. It is known to Bhoja's *Śṛṅgāraprakāśa*, which must be almost contemporary, if the text is not interpolated.

[2] Ed. Bombay, 1899, Pischel, *Die Hofdichter des Lakṣmaṇasena*, pp. 17 ff.; trs. Arnold, *Indian Poetry* (London, 1890), but much more effectively by Rückert, *Abhandlungen für die Kunde des Morgenlandes*, i.

[3] His *Pavanadūta* is ed. Chintaharan Chakravarti, Calcutta, 1926.

[4] Cf. Keith, *Sanskrit Drama*, p. 40.

music. It has been suggested that the presence of end and middle rime, as well as the Yamakas common to Sanskrit poetry, is a proof of origination from an Apabhraṁśa version, but it would be wrong to imagine that the poem had any popular model. It is instead a most elaborate and in its way perfect work of art, and it owes this result largely to the remarkable beauty of the Sanskrit language, with which Apabhraṁśa cannot compare. Jayadeva is a master of form and diction, and above all he is not merely of remarkable skill in metre, but he is able to blend sound to emotion in a manner that renders any effort to represent his work in translation utterly inadequate.

The theme is simple and popular; the estrangement of Kṛṣṇa from his well-beloved Rādhā, while he sports merrily with other maidens in the dance; Rādhā's longing for him; his gradual return to her; and finally the joy of their reunion. Every emotion of Indian love is touched upon—longing, jealousy, hope, disappointment, anger, reconciliation and fruition; the beauty of nature is blended with human love; Jayadeva sings of the spring moonlight which pierces the shadows of the groves, of incense-bearing winds, and of the song of the birds in praise of the omnipotence of the god of love; he depicts the perfection of Indian beauty and transforms into poetry all the arts of love which the *Kāmaśāstra* lays down. There is nothing, we must admit, of the divine in Kṛṣṇa save an occasional reminder that he is the almighty one who removes the sorrows of the world, and it is an idle fancy which sees in the sports of the god with the maidens the entry of the soul into the confusion and incoherence of the manifold, whence he emerges to the love of Rādhā, the bliss of the absolute unity. To Jayadeva the myth of Kṛṣṇa is a living reality, accepted by the popular belief, perhaps by himself also, and the love of the god for Rādhā and his temporary infidelity is but the reflex of the love of man. If the love of Kṛṣṇa and Rādhā in the popular legend has a deeper meaning, it equally has it for Jayadeva, but in no higher degree; in Kālidāsa and in Jayadeva alike, the first great classical Brahmanical writer and the last poet of high accomplishment, we have no effort to present the deeper issues of life and being to our gaze.

Jayadeva's style is worthy of high praise; now in a rapid

flow of short words, now in the more measured movement of long and skilfully constructed compounds, the poem brings home in a series of brilliant pictures the emotions it seeks at once to describe, and to arouse as sentiments in the hearts of its readers or hearers. Of striking effect is the use of the refrain in the songs, which thus are knit together into effective wholes, in place of falling apart into a series of distinct thoughts:

Softly sounds his flute, moved by his breath, and sends thee loving greeting; gladly would he praise the dust, borne by the wind, that touches thy body. In the cool stream, amidst the forest glade, crowned with woodland flowers he dwells.

When a bird moves or a leaf rustles, he deems he hears thy coming, makes ready thy couch, and with timid eye watches the path for thine advent. In the cool stream, amidst the forest glade, crowned with woodland flowers he dwells.

Rādhā, however, cannot seek Kṛṣṇa out in his abode; her strength fails, and her friend must go to urge the lover to seek her in her leafy bower:

Wherever she gazes she sees but thee, with the honey on thy lips. O Hari, O saviour; Rādhā lies there in her bower.

She raises herself to seek thee, but sinks back again, a few steps taken. O Hari, O saviour; Rādhā lies there in her bower.

Flowers and leaves she weaves into chains; longing for thee, she lives but on the memory of thee. O Hari, O saviour; Rādhā lies there in her bower.

'Why speeds not Hari to the place we appointed?' ever she asks her friend. O Hari, O saviour; Rādhā lies there in her bower.

Often she grasps and kisses the shadow, cloud-shaped, deeming it Hari come to her. O Hari, O saviour; Rādhā lies there in her bower.

The end is attainment of the satisfaction of passionate love, akin to that ardour in which the Tantras see the consummation of the effort to unite oneself with the divine, but clothed here in the beauties of Sanskrit poetry:

Press close to my breast in warm embrace the cup of thy bosom through which sweeps the torrent of thy passion; still thus the fire of thy heart. Just for a moment come to him that seeks thee, come to the god, O Rādhā.

Let me drink the nectar of thy lips; awake me from death unto life, thy slave whom the sorrows of separation have pierced with flames of remorse. Just for a moment come to him that seeks thee, come to the god, O Rādhā.

Jayadeva praises himself for his elegance of composition, and for the sentiment expressed by, as well as the beauty and music of, his diction, and for once the praise he arrogates is fully due. The numerous commentaries and imitations attest his deserved fame; without knowing more of his models we cannot be assured what measure of originality to ascribe to him in his choice of form, but we may justly suspect that he practically created the genre. Almost all else that we have of him is a tiny Hindī eulogy of Hari Govind, which is preserved in the *Ādi Granth* of the Sikhs.

The gnomic spirit flows over into the Sanskrit lyric, but it finds also its expression in many other aspects of Sanskrit literature; such stanzas appear already in the Vedic literature, as in the story of Śunaḥśepa in the *Aitareya Brāhmaṇa*, where they are quoted in the midst of prose as normal later; they abound in the law-books and, of course, in the epic, the repository of all Brahmanical lore, and the beast fable is full of these saws which sound quaintly in the mouth of the tigers, apes, venerable birds, and even treacherous cats and foolish asses. An early collection, which exists in many different forms, is the *Cāṇakya Nītiśāstra*,[1] maxims passed off as the outpourings of heart of the great minister of Candragupta, to whom also has been attributed, doubtless with equal inexactitude, the *Arthaśāstra*, to the sad confusion of Indian literary and philosophical chronology. The verses are rather tediously flat, like all proverbial philosophy from Semonides to Martin Tupper; one isolated and rare verse would be interesting, if we could believe that it was aimed at Greeks, and not, as most probable, the Muhammadans; its faulty construction is against an early date. 'The thousands of Caṇḍālas and the sages who see the truth are agreed regarding the Yavana alone; there is none lower than the Yavana.'

Much higher is the value of the *Nītiśataka* of Bhartṛhari, though here again a gentlemanly good sense and prudence, slightly reminiscent of Horace, are the chief characteristics of the saws invented or collected by the amiable if inconstant author:

It is easy to satisfy one who is ignorant, even easier to satisfy a connoisseur; but not the creator himself can please the man who has just a morsel of knowledge.

To hell with caste, and even lower still, let all the virtues go; let

[1] See O. Kressler, *Stimmen indischer Lebensklugheit* (Leipzig, 1907).

conduct fall from the mountain top, let high birth be burned with the fire; heroism is an enemy, let the thunderbolt smite it down. But let wealth be ours, wealth without which all these things are but as a blade of grass.

Those are noble creatures who forget themselves to think of others; the commonalty do good only in so far as is possible without loss to self; those are demons who do injury that they may reap profit therefrom; but what can we call those who do evil without any motive?

Apply what test you will to a man of courage, his constancy will never be false to itself. Turn over the fire; none the less the flame will mount upwards.

There is much good sense in the *Śambhalīmata*[1] of Dāmodaragupta, who lived under Jayāpīḍa of Kashmir (A.D. 779–813), though the work itself, a manual for courtesans, is largely of questionable content and value. Nevertheless we learn:

Those who do not know the dress, manners, and language of other countries and do not pay their respects to learned men are oxen without horns.

That men cling to base women is the fruit of ancient deeds of evil, but women of noble family are the source of happiness for mortals, true companions in joy and sorrow.

In the eleventh century we have similar types of composition in the *Samayamātṛkā*, *Cārucaryā* and *Kalāvilāsa* of the polymath Kṣemendra, whose ability is much more effectively displayed thus than in his more ambitious efforts at condensing the epics or even the *Bṛhatkathā*.

Of far greater importance, however, are treatises giving series of extracts, arranged more or less effectively under subject headings.[2] One of these, certainly, by reason of the palæography of the manuscript, not later than A.D. 1200, is the *Kavīndravacanasamuccaya*; a second, of A.D. 1205,[3] the *Saduktikarṇāmṛta* of Śrīdharadāsa, son of Vaṭudāsa; a third, of the fourteenth century, the *Śārṅgadharapaddhati*[4] of Śārṅgadhara; and a fourth, the *Subhāṣitāvali*[5] (fifteenth century) of Vallabhadeva, contains selections from about 350 poets, as against 264 in the *Śārṅgadharapaddhati* and 446 in

[1] Or *Kuṭṭanīmata*; ed. *Kāvyamālā*, iii, 32 ff.

[2] For a list see Thomas, *Kavīndravacanasamuccaya*, pp. 10 ff.

[3] For the date see *Indian Historical Quarterly*, iii, 188. Ed. *Bibl. Ind.*, 1912 ff.

[4] Ed. *Bombay Sanskrit Series*, No. 37.

[5] Ed. *Bombay Sanskrit Series*, No. 31.

the *Saduktikarṇāmṛta*, which draws especially on works from Bengal. The number of anthologies known is very great, showing the popularity of these excerpts. The value of the attributions of stanzas is probably not very high; there are constant variations from anthology to anthology, and in many cases we can prove errors from the texts we have. The vagueness and inaccuracy are only what must be expected, when it is remembered how difficult it must have been effectively to assign verses to their original authors and how easily tradition was corrupted in the handing down of the original authorities.

The verses thus preserved are often of high merit, revealing to us also the work of authors otherwise but names; to them must be added the citation of many other verses in the works on poetics, whose authors in some cases, as with Bhāmaha and Udbhaṭa, invent their own examples, in others, as in the *Sarasvatīkaṇṭhābharaṇa* and *Śṛṅgāraprakāśa* of Bhoja and Kṣemendra's *Kavikaṇṭhābharaṇa* and *Aucityavicāracarcā*, cite other authors. To Pāṇini,[1] a poet whose grammatical lapses forbid identification with the sage who enunciated the rules of Sanskrit grammar, are attributed some pretty verses:

So close hath the moon, flushed with passion, embraced the face of night, her rolling stars, that in her love she hath not noted that her mantle of darkness hath slipped down to her feet.

He whose glory none may scorn hath reached his setting, as if to proclaim to the man who hath put far from him the fear of death, 'All that hath arisen must pass away, even as I now.'

To this Pāṇini we learn were attributed the *Pātālavijaya* and the *Jāmbavatīvijaya*, and from the verses preserved he must have been no mean poet.

Many notes are struck in these great storehouses, among whose contents are to be found some of the finest lines of Sanskrit literature; a few must suffice to indicate the varied style and manner of this miniature painting of the poets:

Whenever a man rises he should ask himself what good he shall do this day, for the sun must soon be gone, bearing with it a part of his life.

Poets alone, and not the common herd, are moved by the sweet notes of poetry; it is the sea that the rays of the moon stir to motion, not the water in wells.

[1] See Peterson, *Subhāṣitāvali*, pp. 54–58; *J.R.A.S.*, 1891, pp. 311–36; Bhandarkar, *J.B.R.A.S.*, xvi, 344.

O well beloved, remember me.—No; I will not remember thee.—But remembrance is the duty of the heart.—But I have no heart left, for thou hast stolen it from me.

Though I have not long served thee, thou wilt not assuredly, O Lord, refuse to save me. Doth not the ambrosia even at the first draught grant deliverance from old age and death?

When I see thee not, I long for the sight of thee; when I see thee, I fear the separation that must come; neither by seeing thee nor by seeing thee not, can happiness be mine.

Blow, O wind, from where my love dwelleth; having touched her, touch me also. This is much for a lover; through this can he endure to live.

O foe of Madhu, I have not thought of thee, I have not praised thee, I have not glorified thee, nor have I held discourse of thee; nay, not even a blade of grass have I offered in faith to thee; yet do thou have pity on me, that have come to thee for thy protection.

The suggestiveness beloved of the theorists is expressed admirably in the simple stanza, which indicates that the departure of her lover means death to the maiden:

Go if thou must, beloved; happy be thy journey, and may I be born again there whither thou hast gone.

An elaborate and not very intelligible *jeu d'esprit* of this sort is the *Vakroktipañcāśikā* of the Kashmirian Ratnākara, author of the *Haravijaya*, in which Śiva and Pārvatī exchange subtle speeches, in the same manner as in the curious opening stanza of the *Mudrārākṣasa* of Viśākhadatta.

The religious lyric[1] has its reflex in the anthologies, and is largely represented by poems, mainly short, of normally uncertain date and authorship, of which thousands are known to exist, and many have been published in such collections as the *Bṛhatstotraratnākara*. The *Mahimnaḥstava* of Puṣpadanta is moderately early if its author is identical with the Puṣpadanta cited in Jayanta's *Nyāyamañjarī*; a hymn to Śiva, it has won the dubious honour of being treated as if it could serve at the same time as a praise of Viṣṇu. Some of the poems fathered on Śaṅkara are of distinct merit and display true religious fervour, and among these anonymous lyrics are to be found many felicitous and beautiful thoughts and expressions; metre and rime not rarely combine to produce artistic and attractive blending of sound and sense. In a tiny octad on a bee there comes as conclusion a brilliant

[1] See Sivaprasad Bhattacharyya, *Indian Historical Quarterly*, i, 340–60.

illustration of the vanity of hope and endeavour in face of destiny:

> The night will pass, the sun will rise, the lotuses will laugh; while thus the bee dreamed in the calyx, the lotus flower, alas, was crushed by an elephant.

There is, indeed, no end to the richness of Sanskrit literature in stanzas which express with effective brevity the facts of human life and illuminate them by carefully chosen similes; the *Hitopadeśa* is no more than a schoolbook, but its author has had the taste to adapt from the great epic two stanzas, each in its way a perfect expression of a pregnant idea:

> Even as log and log meet for a moment on the mighty ocean, and meeting part again, so are the unions of mortals.
>
> As the streams of the rivers go on, nor ever return, so day and night bear ever away the life of mortals.

On this note it is fitting to end, for it is characteristic of Sanskrit poetry. Life we are permitted to enjoy, we may drink deep of the pleasures of love, but we must not seek to fight against the overmastering power of fate. Had, indeed, fate been outside of us, had it been an alien power, the Indian might have seen that man's duty permitted him to defy it in pursuit of his own ideals, but fate is nothing else than the destiny which has been decreed for one by the deeds of past lives through time without beginning. To strive against destiny is thus meaningless, and Sanskrit poetry loses thus the possibility of the beauty which is implicit in the tragedy of the struggle of man's spirit against powers, which avail to destroy him but not to deprive him of his constancy. As the Indian drama knows no true tragedy, so Indian poetry lacks any such motive, and it lacks also the charm which may be won from a poet's endeavour to interpret nature and human life in the light which appears only to the eyes of the visionary. The possibility of the noblest poetry was thus forbidden, but we may justly recognise that there remained open a field in which much could be accomplished of universal appeal and abiding worth, and that in its richness and beauty of form and sound Sanskrit presented a medium worthy of the highest flights to which any poet could soar.

X

THEORIES OF POETRY

On the history of the theory of poetics we have, as usual in all matters historical in India, no accurate information. A very late source names Kāśyapa and Vararuci among the pioneers of the study; Kāśyapa is a mere name, but, as we have seen, Vararuci is credited with a Kāvya in the *Mahābhāṣya* and many verses are extant in the anthologies under that name, but hardly applicable, we may suspect, to this work. We are thus without any knowledge of the beginnings of the doctrine; the oldest text which deals with the question, the *Bhāratīya Nāṭyaśāstra*, is of uncertain date, but probably somewhat anterior to Bhāsa and Kālidāsa, and the text shows many signs of confusion, re-duplication, and interpolation. Further, it is not concerned with a general theory of poetics, but with the drama. Thanks, however, to this connection, it contains a vital element, which, though neglected for a time, was to come forward decisively later: the doctrine of sentiment.[1] In essence the principle distinguishes between the emotions ascribed to the hero and other characters in the play, and the sentiment (*rasa*) which the seeing of the play evokes in the mind of the spectator. There are eight dominant or abiding feelings or emotions (*sthāyi-bhāva*) love, laughter, sorrow, anger, energy, fear, repugnance, and astonishment; they are contrasted in their abiding character with the transient emotions (*vyabhicāri-bhāva*) which are subordinate to them. The emotions are excited by factors (*vibhāva*), which later definition distinguishes as objects of (*ālambana*), and matters which enflame (*uddīpana*), the emo-

[1] M. Lindenau, *Beiträge zur altindischen Rasalehre;* Regnaud, *La Rhétorique Sanskrite;* H. Jacobi, *Z.D.M.G.*, lvi, 392 ff.; Keith, *Sanskrit Drama*, pp. 314 ff.

tion; thus in the case of love the beloved and the spring fulfil these two functions. They manifest themselves in a large variety of ways (*anubhāva*), a separate class being made of those external manifestations of emotion, such as fainting, which immediately present the working of emotion in a sensitive heart (*sāttvika*). The sentiment is the condition produced in the spectator, and is a single feeling, which is distinguished according to the nature of the emotion by which it is excited into eight classes, but is essentially one, a fact which, of course, entirely differentiates it from an emotion proper. Moreover, it is essentially pleasant, while only some emotions are of this character. Thus the sentiment of fear is a condition of joy; the emotion is the reverse; the one is an ideal condition, the other real. The eight sentiments are that of love (*śṛṅgāra*), the comic (*hāsya*), pathos (*karuṇa*), horror (*raudra*), heroism (*vīra*), fear (*bhayānaka*), disgust (*bībhatsa*), and wonder (*adbhuta*); the sentiment of resignation (*śānta*) is only accepted by later writers, while some added friendship, religious devotion, and faith, though these were rejected for no better ground than their omission from the *Nāṭyaśāstra.* The sentiment was produced in some manner through the emotion by the operation of the factors and consequences, but the delicate point of the mode of production was left undetermined by the *Nāṭyaśāstra.* To sentiment other resources of poetry are subordinate in the *Nāṭyaśāstra,* which mentions ten qualities (*guṇa*) of style, ten defects (*doṣa*), and explains and illustrates the four figures, metaphor (*rūpaka*), simile (*upamā*), the employment of a single predicate for more subjects than one and allied usages (*dīpaka*), and alliteration or repetition of syllables (*yamaka*).

Our earliest authorities on poetry generally are Daṇḍin and Bhāmaha,[1] over whose relative priority an unsettled controversy is yet in process. The essential fact is that both evidently dealt with theories current in their time, but that it is impossible to prove definitely that either borrowed from or attacked the other, since in the case of both we may assume that the criticism is addressed against some earlier exponent of the view disapproved. In the case of Bhāmaha

[1] His work is ed. K. P. Trivedī, App. VIII to his ed. of *Pratāparudrayaśobhūṣaṇa*, Bombay, 1909.

we know he had a precessor in Medhāvin, and, therefore, it is quite impossible to prove that Daṇḍin used Bhāmaha; it is very important to note that he never alludes to one of the verses actually composed by Bhāmaha himself to illustrate his rules. On the other hand, Bhāmaha combats views which Daṇḍin has, and there is some external evidence against an early date for him. He is, in fact, certainly later than the Nyāya philosopher, Uddyotakara, and it is impossible to deny that he cites the *Nyāsa* of Jinendrabuddhi, which may be dated about A.D. 700. The earliest person to whom he is known is Udbhaṭa, who commented on him under Jayāpīḍa of Kashmir (A.D. 779–813). Daṇḍin cannot safely be placed so late; the view that he knew the *Vākyapadīya*[1] of Bhartṛhari is unproven, for we have no evidence that the doctrine common to both is one invented by Bhartṛhari, and his political references suit better a period when the empire of the Guptas had fallen and had not been replaced by that of Harṣa. Daṇḍin therefore may still probably rank as the first of poetic writers extant; the treatment of figures in the *Bhaṭṭi-kāvya*, which is in many regards similar to that of Bhāmaha, is of uncertain date, and very possibly not earlier than about A.D. 641.

At any rate, the *Kāvyādarśa*[2] of Daṇḍin shows us a very simple stage of development of the conception of poetry. The body of poetry is a word-sequence with the sense to be expressed as the determinant, and three forms of poetry are recognised—verse, prose or mixed—as in the drama and the Campū. The highest form of the verse composition is the Sargabandha or Mahākāvya; it should begin with a benediction or salutation or statement of the subject matter; its topic should be one taken from tradition or otherwise real; the end attained should be one of the four great aims of man—profit, duty, desire or release; the hero should be clever and noble; it should contain as ornaments descriptions of a city, the sea, a mountain, the seasons, sunrise, moonrise, sport in the garden or the water, drinking scenes, love passages, feasts, separation or wedding of lovers, the birth of a son, a council, an embassy, a march, a battle, or the victory of the hero; it

[1] iii, 45 (divisions of action); Daṇḍin, ii, 240.
[2] Ed. and trs. S. K. Belvalkar, Poona, 1924.

should not be concise, but should manifest sentiment and feelings. The cantos should not be too long, the metres should be attractive, with a change at the close, and the transition should be neat. Such a poem, suitably ornamented with figures, may last for an age. All these merits are not essential, if the result be still pleasing; it is especially satisfactory to set out the merits of both the hero and his foe and show the hero victorious. The description is admirable as a representation of fact.

Prose poems are divided by custom into two classes, Ākhyāyikā and Kathā, but Daṇḍin decisively rejects the distinction which rests only on externals, the fact that in the former the chapters are styled Ucchvāsa, in the latter Lamba or Lambha[1] is negligible; the other distinctions are contrary to fact; thus in the Ākhyāyikā not only the hero, but another, may narrate, and the distinction that the metres Vaktra and Aparavaktra occur in the Ākhyāyikā and Āryā only in the Kathā is incorrect. There is no essential distinction in subject matter between these forms of the prose poem.

Four languages may be used in poetry; Sanskrit, Prākrit, Apabhraṁśa, i.e. the speech of the Ābhīras and others, and a mixture of these; the Sargabandha is in Sanskrit, thus ignoring Prākrit Kāvyas; but the Kathā can be in Sanskrit or in any dialect, while a mixture is used in dramas.

There are many types of style, but only two need be distinguished, the Vaidarbha and the Gauḍa, which are generally opposed.[2] The first has the ten qualities alluded to in the *Nāṭyaśāstra*, which are here described as the breath of poetry. They are a somewhat confused set; two of them demand perspicuity and clearness (*arthavyakti*, *prasāda*); five refer to sound effects, firm structure (*śleṣa*), sweetness (*mādhurya*), gentleness (*sukumāratā*), sameness or evenness of sounds (*samatā*), and strength (*ojas*), defined as multitude of compounds in prose as opposed to verse; elevation (*udāratva*) in the sense of the expression of some high merit, or the use of poetic phrases such as a bracelet of gold; grace or beauty (*kānti*), and metaphorical expressions (*samādhi*). The last is

[1] Derived doubtless from Lambhaka in the *Bṛhatkathā*.

[2] Vāmana accepts the Pāñcāla, which is marked by gentleness and sweetness, and the *Sāhityadarpaṇa* the Lāṭa, intermediate between Vaidarbha and Pāñcāla. The details are of no interest.

said to be the whole of poetry. Natural genius, much study, and constant practice are the requisites for the highest art; but, if the first be absent, much may be done by the other two. These topics are followed in Books II and III of the *Kāvyādarśa* by an elaborate discussion of the figures of sense and of sound, but there is no attempt to define figures beyond assigning to them the function of beautifying a poem, The question of sentiment seems thus neglected, but this is not wholly the case; the quality of sweetness is described as the permanence of sentiment in subject and expression, and certain figures are said to convey sentiment.

Of historical interest is the treatment of the Gauḍa style by Daṇḍin, for it marks a definite advance over the *Nāṭyaśāstra*; the chief characteristics assigned to it are the use of long compounds even in verse, love of alliteration, readiness to admit harsh effects and intermingling of different classes of sounds, etymologising, bombast, and exaggeration. The doctrine of Daṇḍin is carried out to a more complete result in Vāmana,[1] who doubtless lived under Jayāpīḍa of Kashmir. Style (*rīti*) becomes the soul of poetry, that is, the element which distinguishes it from such a lifeless thing as a philosophical treatise. Style, again, is diction distinguished by the qualities, and is of three kinds: Vaidarbha which has all, Gauḍīya which has strength and beauty, and Pāñcāla which has sweetness and gentleness. The qualities thus are made the causes of charm (*śobhā*) in a poem, a function ascribed by Daṇḍin to the figures, and the latter are reduced to the function of heightening the qualities. A further change of importance is the finding of a new place for the expression of sentiment in the qualities; it is included under the elements of beauty, whereas Daṇḍin found place for it under sweetness and the figures Preyas, Rasavat, and Ūrjasvin. Again, Daṇḍin includes as a figure Bhāvika, which is the poetic expression of any idea without the use of metaphorical terms (*vakrokti*), and Vāmana sensibly resolves this into the appropriate qualities. These he classifies as qualities of sound and sense, and in this he is undoubtedly pedantic, as he has to make unconvincing distinctions in order to have two sets each of ten qualities.

[1] His *Kāvyālaṁkāra*, with his own comm., is ed. *Kāvyamālā*, No. 15; trs. *Indian Thought*, iii and iv.

An important step towards simplification was made in the doctrine of styles by Udbhaṭa, when under the name of Vṛtti, manners, he distinguished the elegant (*upanāgarikā*), the ordinary (*grāmyā*), and the harsh (*paruṣā*), the distinctions being based on the sound effects only, thus ignoring other forms of qualities. Hence we have in Mammaṭa[1] the adoption of a threefold enumeration of qualities based only on sound effects as reflecting conditions of consciousness; all the other seven of Vāmana's list are reduced to these three—sweetness, strength, and clearness. Sweetness arises from the use of nasals with the unaspirated mutes corresponding (save in the case of the lingual), *r* and *ṇ* with short vowels, no compounds or short compounds; strength from the use of linguals, compounds of the same letter or of a letter and its aspirated form, *r* compounded, *ś* and *ṣ*, and long compounds; clearness is when the mere sound suggests the sense. The qualities of sense are thus ignored.

Bhāmaha supplies us with a different conception of the essence of poetry, in that he lays stress on the element of metaphorical or poetic speech (*vakrokti*), suggesting that hyperbole (*atiśayokti*) lies at the bottom of all poetic expression. The distinction of quality and figure is obscured in him as in Daṇḍin; he also has the figure Bhāvika, which is a really striking presentation of an object through the exercise of the imagination. We have here the pregnant idea of a figure as resting on poetic vision, but the necessity of sentiment in a poem is not admitted. Neither Udbhaṭa[2] nor Pratīhārendurāja, who commented on him (A.D. 950), made any noteworthy advance on him.

An important, if not entirely new, doctrine, however, was expounded about A.D. 820 by the Dhvanikāra, whose 120 Kārikās have come down to us with the Āloka of Ānanda-

[1] Probably from Bhaṭṭa Nāyaka, who makes sweetness correspond to a melting (*druti*), clearness to an extension (*vistara*), and strength to an expansion (*vikāsa*) of the movement of consciousness. Three qualities only are already accepted by Bhāmaha (ii, 1–3), which suggests posteriority to Daṇḍin. See also *Sāhityadarpaṇa*, viii; *Kāvyaprakāśa*, pp. 537 ff.

[2] His apparent reference to sentiment (vi, 17) is explained away by Sovani, *Bhandarkar Comm. Vol.*, p. 391. Ed. *Bombay Sanskrit and Prākrit Series*, No. 79.

vardhana, written perhaps forty years later, and the further exposition of the philosopher, Abhinavagupta (A.D. 1000). This doctrine, while not without rivals, by its adoption by Mammaṭa attained the premier position in Indian poetics; its origin in close connection with grammatical studies is proved by the singular term, Dhvani, tone, used to describe it. The grammarians, as opposed to the philosophers in general, assumed the existence of an ideal entity, Sphoṭa, which was revealed by the uttering of the sound of a word, bringing to the mind the sense of the term.[1] Similarly, in a poem what is expressed brings up something unexpressed, and of much greater importance in true poetry, which then may be styled Tone. The basis of the doctrine can be seen in the doctrine of the meaning of words, which was the object both of grammatical and philosophical study. The primary meaning of a word was obviously to convey a direct sense, but also obviously many terms in ordinary usage were metaphorical (*lakṣaṇika*), as in the phrase, 'The tribunal is glad,' where the people composing it are meant; or 'A herdsmen's station on the Ganges,' which must denote on the Ganges' bank. But such terms have no special grace for poetry; those appeal only which are chosen by the genius of the poet for his purpose (*prayojana*), and, if we investigate why phrases are chosen, as when wine is called the milk of the aged, we see that the poet thus intends, without actually expressing it, to bring to our minds the invaluable qualities of milk. The same power of suggestion (*vyañjanā*) is possible in the case of words which, without being metaphorical, have double senses, and of whole sentences or works. The theory, therefore, holds that the power of suggestion or Dhvani is the soul of a poem, and not as did Vāmana the style. It transferred, it may be said, the importance of a poem to the suggested matter or content, not to the expressed content, which is regarded as of inferior value to the unexpressed. We must draw a distinction between æsthetic pleasure and ordinary feeling. A man feels pleasure in the ordinary sense

[1] Keith, *Indian Logic and Atomism*, p. 163, n. 4; Jacobi, *Z.D.M.G.*, lvi, 399; Liebich, *Z.D.M.G.*, lxxvii, 208 ff.; Abegg, *Festschrift Windisch*, pp. 88 ff. The text is ed. *Kāvyamālā*, No. 25, 1911. No certain result as to the authorship has been attained; cf. A. Sankaran, *Third Or. Conference*, pp. 85 ff.

if one says to him, 'I shall give you a valuable gift,' but that is not the feeling which is excited by true poetry. That is something supernormal (*alaukika*), an æsthetic pleasure (*camatkāra*), which we understand, because we actually experience it and are conscious of it, but which cannot be explained in any other terms. The pleasure is comparable to the appreciation of unity with the absolute attained in meditation by the adept; it is something which comes to the man of taste (*sahṛdaya*), and if a man has not taste—as a result of misdeeds in a former birth—he cannot experience the feeling.

What is suggested only, and not expressed, may be a thought or subject matter (*vastu*), or a figure (*alaṁkāra*), or normally a sentiment (*rasa*). The importance of sentiment is now fully appreciated, and the mode in which poetry or a drama affects the reader or spectator can now be better understood. The appreciation of sentiment cannot come by any process of inference; it is possible only because a man has in the past had experiences, e.g. of love, which have left residues in the shape of impressions in his soul. When he comes under the influence of the factors which excite these emotions and their consequences, expressed in poetry or on the stage, he does not regard them as external, as proper to the hero of the work, nor as personal to himself; he appreciates them as universal, and he shares in them in this manner, enjoying a strange pleasure, even when the emotions of the hero in the work are painful. The form given to the conception is sometimes obscure and difficult, but the attempt to express the essential character of the pleasure of poetry is daring and by no means ineffective.

A threefold division of poetry is laid down. The first class is that in which the suggested sense is superior to the expressed content of the work; the second that in which, while suggestion is present, the expressed content is superior to that suggested, and suggestion is thus only a secondary element (*guṇībhūtavyaṅgya*) in the poem; thirdly we have 'picture (*citra*)' poems, which have no element of suggestion at all, a concession made obviously to popular opinion, which gave the title of poetry to works which relied on the expressed meaning only. The first class was variously sub-divided; the suggestion may rest on the figurative sense (*lakṣaṇā*) of words, or on the literal sense, and in the latter case we have a distinction between the cases where the effect of suggestion is immediate, as in a drama, or where the procedure which leads up to the suggestion is discernible. The further subdivisions are unimportant, but it is to be noted that, in cases where the suggestion is immediate and it falls short of the expressed sense in beauty, we have the figures of speech known as Rasavat, Preyas, Ūrjasvin, and so on,[1] and the poem belongs to the second class in which the suggested meaning is inferior to the expressed.

The relation of the qualities and the figures is now said to be that the qualities support the suggested content which is the soul of the poem, while the figures perform a similar function for the body of the poem, since they adorn either the sense or the sound. It is clear on this view that there is an essential distinction between the qualities and the figures, which cannot be equated in any way. In the detailed discussion of style there are many remarks of interest; qualities are reduced to three—sweetness, strength, and clearness—and an effort is made to lay down the principles on which compounds should be used. Where sentiment is to be suggested, it is necessary to be specially careful in the use of language. It is absurd to use long compounds in the drama, and, while such compounds befit the Ākhyāyikā, they are out of place there in cases where pathos and sorrow in love are to be suggested, and in the Kathā greater moderation in compounds is appropriate.

An effort to simplify the theory of Tone is found in Abhinavagupta, where the matter suggested is reduced to sentiment alone, to the exclusion of figures or thought; that these can be suggested is true, but in the long run they rest on the suggestion of sentiment.[2] So in Mammaṭa's *Kāvyaprakāśa*[3] we find the qualities and the figures related to the sentiment only, the first as supporting it, the latter as embellishing the sense and sound, which make up the body of which sentiment is the soul. But this view, which is also accepted by the author of the *Sāhityadarpaṇa*, Viśvanātha, in the fourteenth century, did not prevail. The great systema-

[1] *Alaṁkārasarvasva*, p. 185.
[2] *Dhvanyālokalocana*, pp. 65, 152.
[3] Frequently ed. *Ānandāśrama Sanskrit Series*, Nos. 66 and 89; Mysore, 1922; trs. G. Jhā, Benares, 1918.

tiser, Jagannātha, in his *Rasagaṅgādhara*, in the seventeenth century, insists that we must admit the existence of poetry where a figure or a thought alone is suggested, and the question of sentiment does not arise; poets have produced works in which the play, for example, of children or of apes is described, and in which it is idle to seek to find sentiment suggested, except on the same principle that any statement of fact may be regarded indirectly as producing sentiment. He falls back, then, on the definition of poetry as sound expressive of a delightful subject matter. He also keeps the third class of poetry where suggestion is absent, and sub-divides it as dependent on sense or on sound, making four great divisions in all.

The doctrine of Tone, however, by no means secured universal assent. About A.D. 900, Bhaṭṭa Nāyaka[1] developed a different theory in special connection with the drama and the nature of sentiment. He denied that it could either be perceived or produced or revealed, and instead insisted that three factors co-operated; the first is the expression in words (*abhidhā*), the second the power of generalising and making real to others which lies in a poem (*bhāvakatva*), and the third the power of the spectator or reader to enjoy (*bhojakatva*). For him the real essence of a poem lies as for the *Nāṭyaśāstra* in the sentiment. On the other hand, Kuntaka or Kuntala before A.D. 1050 revived the doctrine of Bhāmaha, which makes the essence of poetry depend on the poet's skill in speech; the *Vakroktijīvita* evidently attained classical rank as the detailed expression of this view. Mahiman Bhaṭṭa, on the other hand, developed, following the doctrine of the earlier Śaṅkuka, the principle that inference was sufficient explanation of the enjoyment of poetry, a subject which he treated at length in the *Vyaktiviveka*,[2] refuting the views of Kuntaka no less than those of the Dhvani school, and being refuted energetically in return by Mammaṭa, whose *Kāvyaprakāśa* was written in conjunction with Allaṭa about A.D. 1100, by Vidyādhara in his *Ekāvalī*[3] (A.D. 1300), by Viśvanātha in the

[1] *Dhvanyālokalocana*, p. 67; *Ekāvalī*, p. 85.

[2] Ed. *Trivandrum Sanskrit Series*, No. 5, 1909, with Ruyyaka's commentary. On Kuntaka see S. K. De, *Sanskrit Poetics*, i, 136 ff., and his ed. of the *Vakroktijīvita*.

[3] Ed. K. P. Trivedī, Bombay, 1903.

Sāhityadarpaṇa, and by Vidyānātha, in his *Pratāparudrayaśobhūṣaṇa*[1] (A.D. 1300). Other writers remained on the basis of the sentiment theory of the *Nāṭyaśāstra*, as do Rudraṭa in his *Kāvyālaṁkāra*,[2] written before 900 A.D., Rājaśekhara in his *Kāvyamīmāṁsā*,[3] written about A.D. 900, and Bhojadeva in the *Sarasvatīkaṇṭhābharaṇa*,[4] which was written for him in the first half of the eleventh century. Hemacandra's *Kāvyānuśāsana*[5] with his comment on it, the *Alaṁkāracūḍāmaṇi* is a mere compilation which uses Mammaṭa, but shows no personal attitude of consequence. The sentiment theory prevails in Rudra Bhaṭṭa's *Śṛṅgāratilaka*[6] probably in the eleventh century, in the famous *Daśarūpa*[7] of Dhanaṁjaya and the *Avaloka* of Dhanika, which deal with the drama, and date from the last quarter of the tenth century, and in the *Rasamañjarī* and the *Rasataraṅgiṇī* of Bhānudatta, before A.D. 1400.

Throughout the literature the importance of figures, especially, as the time passes, of those of sense, is recognised, and elaborate efforts are made more precisely to define the various figures. For a really systematic treatment, however, we must go to Ruyyaka of Kashmir, who, in addition to commenting on the *Kāvyaprakāśa* of Mammaṭa and Allaṭa in the *Kāvyaprakāśasaṁketa*, wrote a number of other works, of which the chief is the *Alaṁkārasarvasva*,[8] a treatise which was not seriously challenged until the appearance of the *Rasagaṅgādhara*[9] of Jagannātha. One chief merit lies in his application to the matter of the scientific form of exposition and examination, which is found applied to the general question of poetics in the *Dhvanyāloka* of Ānandavardhana, and the effort scientifically to classify and explain the bases of the figures. According to the Kashmirian tradition, preserved in the commentary of Jayaratha, written in the early part of

[1] Ed. K. P. Trivedī, Bombay, 1909.
[2] Ed. *Kāvyamālā*, No. 2, 1886.
[3] Ed. Baroda, 1916.
[4] Ed. Calcutta, 1884.
[5] Ed. *Kāvyamālā*, No. 71, 1901.
[6] Ed. R. Pischel, Kiel, 1886.
[7] Ed. and trs. G. C. O. Haas, New York, 1912.
[8] Ed. *Kāvyamālā*, No. 35, 1893; *Trivandrum Sanskrit Series*, No. 40, 1915.
[9] Ed. *Kāvyamālā*, No. 12, 1888.

the thirteenth century, less than a hundred years after the work, both the rules and the Vṛtti on them are by Ruyyaka; in the southern tradition, preserved in the comment of Samudrabandhu, the Vṛtti is by Maṅkhuka or Maṅkhaka, the poet and pupil of Ruyyaka. We need not disregard the tradition, which dates before A.D. 1300, or take it too literally; what is meant is doubtless that Maṅkhaka aided his teacher in the production of the work. Compared with it little value attaches to such texts as the *Vāgbhaṭālaṁkāra*[1] of Vāgbhaṭa, son of Soma, who wrote under Jayasiṁha of Aṇhilvāḍ (A.D. 1093–1143), or the *Candrāloka*[2] of the dramatist and logician Jayadeva (*c.* A.D. 1200), which does not seem to make use of Ruyyaka's work.

In Ruyyaka we find a general defence of the views of the Dhvani school on poetry and, what is more important, a clear perception of the nature of poetic figures.[3] This is charm (*vicchitti*), which essentially distinguishes ordinary works, such as treatises on logic, from poetry. There is, for instance, the figure, doubt; it is quite distinct from the mere problem, 'Is this a post or a man?' which is doubt arising from the circumstances; to be a figure it must be a doubt raised by the imagination (*pratibhā*) of the poet. This criterion is rigidly applied by Jagannātha, who condemns certain alleged figures, because they have no charm at all. To define charm is obviously impossible; the *Nāṭyaśāstra*[4] contains an illustration of it by comparing it with the elegant wearing of garlands, clothes, ornaments, and pigments, and nothing better is made of it later. The inspiration of the poet is recognised equally as incapable of precise definition. It was an old idea, for we have it in the Buddhist scriptures in the sense of the power of composition of impromptu verses, and we meet the very curious discrimination of poets as those by reflection, those by study, those by subject matter, and those by inspiration.[5] The theorists from the first are singularly emphatic in the recognition of the necessity of inspiration to

[1] Ed. *Kāvyamālā*, No. 48, 1895.

[2] Part of this text is worked up by Appayya Dikṣita (*c.* A.D. 1600) in his *Kuvalayānanda Kārikās*.

[3] See H. Jacobi, *Gött. Nach.*, 1908, pp. 1 ff.

[4] xxii, 16.

[5] *Aṅguttara Nikāya*, ii, 230.

make a poet. They recognise the value of study and practice, but they know that without the former qualification neither of the other two requisites can effect the desired end. Abhinavagupta describes it as the capacity to create something new, and gives as its characteristics the ability to produce sentiment, clearness, beauty, and poetry.

The demand for constant practice takes on diverse shapes; Hemacandra,[1] for instance, gives an ascending series of four forms in which imitation may be carried out as an exercise in improvement of poetic skill, and he even allows the use of three lines of a stanza, though to take four is pure theft, and, while by the passage of time an ordinary theft may be blotted out, that of poetry passes to the next generation. We have here a sign of the elaborate cultivation of the poetic art, which is seen in the constant effort of the poets to put old ideas in slightly varied shape. Poetry was ruled by convention (*saṁgati*), and a large number of ideas[2] are commonplaces which appear naturally everywhere; fame is white and so is laughter; the darkness can be grasped; the evil man is two-tongued like the serpent, and there is poison on his lips; the blue lotus opens to the rays of the sun, and bemoans its setting; the nails of kings are polished on the jewels of the coronets of subject princes; the Aśoka is without flower or fruit, and is made to blossom by the touch of a maiden's foot; the Cātaka bird is so proud that it will drink only the water of the cloud; fate severs the Cakravāka birds during the night, which they spend in sorrowful cries; the moon is the beloved of the Cakora which imbibes its rays as a lover drinks in with his eyes the radiance of his beloved's countenance, and so on. In the hands of third-rate poets, such as Vidyādhara and Vidyānātha, in the illustrations they supply to their works on poetics, the whole thing is banal and tedious, but the theorists never forgot that genius was necessary for the highest poetry, as they show by the extraordinary fondness they show for citing Kālidāsa, and the premier rank they assign to him.

The aims of a poet are normally given as fame and pleasure, but Bhāmaha already includes the full four ends of man—profit, pleasure, virtue, and release. The attainment of wealth,

[1] See also Kṣemandra, *Kavikaṇṭhābharaṇa*, i, 20; ii, 1.
[2] See Rājaśekhara *Kāvyamīmāṁsā*, xiv–xvi.

social accomplishment, escape from ill, and instruction are also given as ends, though both Vāgbhaṭa and Hemacandra observe that some of these aims can be attained by other means, and therefore are not peculiar to poetry. The poets are very distinctly conscious that they win not merely renown for themselves, but also for their patrons. The sentiment of Daṇḍin[1] is admirably expressed by an unknown writer in the *Subhāṣitāvali:*[2]

> Where now are the hundreds of loads of gold, where the troop of rutting elephants, which the might of Harṣa bestowed on the merit of Bāṇa? But the glory conferred on him by Bāṇa's flow of speech will, I ween, fade not even when the æon passes away.

If, however, the poets looked to kings as their most generous patrons in return for a friendship far more precious than anything else, they expected appreciation from the man of taste (*rasika*) or of heart (*sahṛdaya*), one who by the possession of a sympathetic nature, as the result of study in this and former births, can appreciate true poetry and make it his own. A true poem[3] stirs the heart like wine, makes the head shake, the cheeks redden, fills the eyes with tears, and stays the voice as it fain would recite its beauties. The poet himself as creator of his work does not enjoy its perfection; it is only when he becomes a spectator that he can feel its loveliness, just as the actor appreciates the drama in which he acts only in so far as he places himself in the position of one of the audience. To attain this perfection of appreciation, this ability to appropriate a poem, is not always possible, even with much study, for it may be that evil deeds done in former births will prevent the enlightenment arising, just as the appreciation of the divinity may not be attained by men whose souls are not purified from evil.

Such a discriminating audience demands, of course, like the Roman audiences of whom Juvenal and Martial tell us, something elaborate; it disdains plain fare, and must have an exquisite morsel to tickle the palate. If we have such a verse as

> Behold, the crane rests yonder motionless and still on the lotus leaf, even as the conch shell on a tray of emerald,

[1] i, 5. Cf. F. W. Thomas, *Bhandarkar Comm. Vol.*, pp. 384 ff.
[2] v, 180.
[3] *Subhāṣitāvali*, 163.

it is valued only because of the hidden meaning it conveys; a maiden thus indicates indirectly to a lover who is near by the safe spot for an assignation.[1] We are thus compelled to seek strained effects in order to satisfy such connoisseurs, to compare an orange for its hue to the fresh-shaved chin of a drunken Hun,[2] and to ransack mythology, grammar, and all the sciences to obtain new and striking, if often tasteless and absurd, similes to lend freshness to worn-out themes. The grotesqueness of much of Sanskrit poetry owes its existence to the constant effort thus to diversify. At the same time, the exaggeration which so often marks learned verse, as in the case of Lucan, is nearly always present, aimed at in the effort to revive the wearied sentiment of wonder and admiration. Moreover, as we have seen, a conventional language is demanded which exacts from every poet the conception of the mountain rocks dripping with the juice of rutting elephants, and of the animal with two r's (*bhramara*), the bee, kissing the flowers and drunk with the honey which it extracts from them. To possess an almost unending supply of such tags was essential for poets who often might be expected to take part in a contest of composing stanzas extempore in the presence of their patrons; such a poet (*āśukavi*, *śīghrakavi*) was an ornament of a Court,[3] and such works as the *Bhojaprabandha*[4] of Ballālasena and the *Prabandhacintāmaṇi*[5] of Merutuṅga show how popular the amusement was. Even the *Kāmasūtra* of Vātsyāyana already ranks the art of making up stanzas, given a line (*kāvyasamasyāpūraṇa*), among the sixty-four accomplishments to be learned by maidens.

[1] *Sāhityadarpaṇa*, 28.
[2] Ibid., 622.
[3] Pischel, *Die Hofdichter des Lakṣmaṇasena*, pp. 27 ff.
[4] Ed. Bombay, 1913.
[5] Ed. Bombay, 1888; trs. C. H. Tawney, Calcutta, 1894-1901.

INDEX

ABDALLAH ibn al Muqaffa', 106
Abhidhā, denotation, 130
Abhinanda, 95
Abhinavagupta, 127, 129, 133
Ābhīras, 124
Aborigines, influence on language, 10
Accent, loss of Vedic, 19
Adbhuta, sentiment of wonder, 122
Æneid, 43
Æsthetic pleasure, 127
Agnivarman, 41
Āhavamalla, 61
Aihole inscription, 48
Aims of the poet, 133, 134
Aitareya Brāhmaṇa, 9, 102, 116
Aja, story of, 22, 38, 39
Ajākṛpāṇīya, 14
Ākhyāna, type of narrative, 83
Ākhyāyikā, 58, 68, 69, 73, 77, 98, 124, 129
Ālambana, 121
Alaṁkāra, man, 54
Alaṁkāra, work, 72
Alaṁkāras, figures, 43, 132, 133
Alaṁkāracūḍāmaṇi, 131
Alaṁkārasarvasva, 131
Alaukika, form of pleasure, 128
Alexandrian poetic style, 49, 52, 74
Allahabad Praśasti, 25, 26
Allaṭa, 130, 131
Alliteration, 24, 26, 50, 56, 61, 72, 74, 75, 78, 81
Āloka, 131
Amaru, Amarūka, 109–12
Ānanda, 23
Ānandavardhana, 37, 68 n. 3, 109, 126–27, 131
Andhaka, legend of, 53
Anthologies, 117–19
Antonius Diogenes, 80
Antyānuprāsa, 56
Anubhāva, consequences, 122
Anwāri Suhailī, 106
Anyoktimuktālatā, 109
Anyoktiśataka, 109
Aorist, 17, 18, 19, 23, 49, 89, 103
Apabhraṁśa, 20, 21, 114, 124
Apaśabda, 12
Appayya Dīkṣita, 132 n. 2
Appreciation of poetry, 134
Āraṇyakas, language of, 8
Ardha-Māgadhī, 10
Arikesarin II, 81
Aristocratic character of Sanskrit literature, 16, 134
Arjuna, 47–49
Arthālaṁkāras, figures of sound, 24, 44
Arthāntaranyāsa, a figure, 45
Arthaśāstra, 97, 98, 116
Arthavyakti, simplicity of style, 25, 124
Artificiality of Sanskrit poetry, 16, 135
Āryā metre, 21
Āryāsaptaśatī, 108
Ārya Śūra, 95
Āryāvarta, 12
Aśoka, king, 10, 62
Aśoka, tree, 31, 133
Assonance, *see* Alliteration *and* Paronomasia
Āśukavi, improviser, 135
Aśvaghoṣa, 13, 14, 15, 16, 18, 20, 21–25, 27, 29, 71, 95
Atharvaveda, 27
Atiśayokti, 126
Aucityavicāracarcā, 118

Austro-Asiatic influence on Sanskrit literature, 10, 38 n. 2
Avadānaśataka, 56, 95
Avaloka, 131
Avantisundarīkathā, 67 n. 2
Avantivarman, 53

BABYLONIKA, 80
Ballālasena, 135
Bāṇa, 16, 18, 25, 54, 59, 66, 75–79, 81, 82, 112
Barzōe, 106
Bauddhasaṁgatyalaṁkāra, 72
Beauty, of style, 25, 124
Bhāmaha, 15, 67, 122, 123, 126, 130, 133
Bhānudatta, 131
Bharata epic, 13
Bhāratamañjarī, 54
Bhāratīya Nāṭyaśāstra, 7, 13, 19, 47, 121, 122, 125, 131, 132
Bhāravi, 17, 23, 48–50, 51, 52, 55, 104 n. 2
Bhartṛhari, 50, 102, 111, 112, 116, 123
Bhāsa, 2, 3, 13, 19, 29, 34, 60, 67, 82, 85, 89 n. 1, 121
Bhāṣā, 9, 10, 11, 17
Bhāskara, 28
Bhaṭṭa Nāyaka, 126 n. 1, 130
Bhaṭṭāra Haricandra, 60, 66
Bhaṭṭi-kāvya, 17, 50, 53, 67, 123
Bhauma, 18
Bhavabhūti, 52
Bhāvakatva, power to generalise, 130
Bhāvika, figure, 125, 126
Bhayānaka, sentiment of fear, 122
Bhīma, 18
Bhīmaratha, story of, 14
Bhoja, Bhojadeva, 16, 82, 113 n. 1, 118, 131
Bhoja, of Kashmir, 64
Bhojakatva, power to enjoy, 130
Bhojaprabandha, 135
Bhūsaṇa Bhaṭṭa, 75, 79
Bībhatsa, sentiment of disgust, 122
Bilhaṇa, 16, 25, 60–62, 63, 112 n. 1, 113
Black Yajurveda, 8
Brāhmaṇas, language of, 8, 9, 15
Brahmanical revival, 43, 99
Brahmins, speech of, 12; satire on, 100, 101
Bṛhaspati, King, 53
Bṛhatkathā, 60, 69, 77, 79, 80, 84–95
Bṛhatkathāmañjarī, 84–86
Bṛhatkathāsaritsāgara, 86
Bṛhatkathāślokasaṁgraha, 28, 84, 86, 89
Būd, 106
Budhasvāmin, 86, 89, 95
Buddha, language of the, 10
Buddhacarita, 21, 23, 24
Buddhist influences, 90, 96, 97, 99, 101, 111, 112; classification of poets, 132

CAKORA, 133
Cakravāka, 133
Cakravartin, motif, 87
Camatkāra, æsthetic pleasure, 128
Campū, 80–83, 123
Cāṇakya, 98
Cāṇakya Nītiśāstra, 116
Caṇḍīśataka, 112 n. 2
Candragupta, Maurya, 116
Candragupta I, 26
Candragupta II, 26, 30, 43
Candrāloka, 132
Candrāpīḍa, 75, 76
Caraka, 15
Cārucaryā, 117
Cārudatta, 67, 88
Cātaka, 133
Caurapañcāśikā, 60, 112
Chandaḥsūtra, 26, 27
Chāndogya Upaniṣad, 96
Chandonuśāsana, 55
Chandoviciti, 67
Character drawing, 38, 39, 63, 77, 78, 89
Characteristics of Sanskrit poetry, 120
Charm, 125
Cippaṭa Jayāpīḍa, 53
Citra, kind of poetry, 128
Clearness, of style, 25, 124, 126

Cloud as messenger, 32
Comic sentiment, 122
Compounds, 17, 18, 24, 25, 26, 34, 35, 56, 68 n. 3, 71, 73, 74, 78, 81, 103, 115, 129
Conventional language in poetry, 133, 135
Court epic, in Kālidāsa, 34–42; after Kālidāsa, 46–56
Culture, 28, 134, 135

DAKṢIṆĀVARTANĀTHA, 34
Damanaka, 99, 106
Damayantīkathā, 81
Dāmodaragupta, 117
Daṇḍin, 18, 25, 46, 47, 55, 66–72, 85, 89, 94, 122–26, 134
Daśakumāracarita, 67, 68, 75
Daśaratha, 40
Daśarūpa, 131
Dattaka Sarvāśraya, 51
Description, 22, 26, 32, 33, 35, 46, 48, 49, 51, 54, 56, 61, 71, 78, 89, 110, 111, 112
Destiny, 120
Deterioration of language, 17
Dhanaṁjaya, 131
Dhanaṁjaya, author of a *Rāghavapāṇḍavīya*, 53 n. 1
Dhanapāla, 79
Dhanika, 131
Dharmakīrti, 72
Dharmaśarmābhudaya, 66, 82 n. 1
Dhavalacandra, 105
Dhoyī, Dhoyīka, 33, 113
Dhvani, theory of suggestion, 126–31
Dhvanikāra, 126–29
Dhvanyāloka, 151
Dialects, absence of, in Sanskrit, 16
Didactic fable, 96–105
Diddā, 63
Dignāga, 30, 45
Dīnāra, 99
Dīpaka, figure, 122
Doni, A. F., 106
Doṣa, defect, 122
Double entendre, *see* Śleṣa
Drama, 13, 14
Dravidian influence on Sanskrit, 19
Dvyāśrayakāvya, 64

EASTERN style, *see* Gauḍa
Ekāvalī, 130
Elevation of style, 25, 124
Emotion, suggestion of, 33, 37, 42, 109, 110; *and see* Sentiment
Epic, language of, 7, 8, 11, 12; influence on Kāvya, 16
Equivoke, *see* Paronomasia
Erotic descriptions, 51, 70
Etymologising, in style, 74, 125
Euphues, 74
Evenness, in style, 124
Exaggeration, in style, 47, 74, 125, 135

FABLES, 96–106
Fate, 64, 120
Fear, sentiment of, 122
Figures, 25, 43, 45, 50, 64, 72, 74, 125, 129, 130, 132, 133
Flying machines, 91
Foreign influence on Sanskrit, 19
Foreign translations of the *Pañcatantra*, 106

GADYACINTĀMAṆI, 79
Gaṇapāṭha, 18
Gaṇḍīstotragāthā, 24
Gāthā language, 11
Gauḍa style, 46, 47, 73, 124, 125
Gaüḍavaha, 52, 61
Genius, necessary in poet, 125, 132
Gentleness, of style, 124
Ghaṭakarpara, 107
Girnar Praśasti, of Rudradāman, 24, 25, 68
Gītagovinda, 113–16
Gnomic verse, 116–20
Gomukha, 88
Govardhana, 108, 113
Govinda, 19
Grammatical irregularities, 16–18, 24, 71, 72, 103
Grāmyā, manner, 126
Greek astrology, 19, 29 n. 1, 79; elegy, 32; historiography, 62;

influence on Sanskrit romance, 79–81; words in Sanskrit, 19
Guṇa, quality, 24, 25, 122, 124, 125, 128, 129
Guṇāḍhya, 77, 84, 85–89, 94, 103
Guṇībhūtavyaṅgya, kind of poetry, 128

HĀLA, 15, 47, 107–109; *and see* Sātavāhana
Halāyudha, 18, 53
Haravijaya, 53, 119
Haricandra, 60, 66, 82
Hariṣeṇa, 25, 26, 68, 83 n. 1
Harṣa, Harṣadeva, 16, 59, 123, 134
Harṣa, Śrī-Harṣa, 17, 55
Harṣacarita, 58, 59, 61, 67, 68, 72, 75, 85, 107
Hekataios, 62
Hemacandra, 55, 64, 65, 89, 95, 105 n. 2, 131, 133, 134
Heroic sentiment, 23, 39, 40, 42, 49, 75, 122
Heron of Alexandria, 80
Hieratic language, 8, 9, 18
Himālaya, 35
Historic Kāvya, 57–65
History in India, 57, 58
Hitopadeśa, 104, 105, 120
Horace, 116
Horror, sentiment of, 122
Humour, 45, 82, 100, 108, 122
Huns, 30, 135
Hyperbole, *see* Exaggeration

IAMBLICHOS, 80
Iliad, 11, 37
Imperfect, use of, 49, 103
Indelicacy, 37, 70, 71
Indra III, 80
Inscriptions, 14, 24–26, 57, 68, 79, 83 n. 1
Inspiration, of poet, 132
Iranian words in Sanskrit, 19
Irregularities of grammar, 16–18, 23, 24
I-Tsing, 111

JĀBĀLI, 75, 76
Jagannātha, 130, 110, 132
Jain authors, 15, 33, 34, 79, 81, 82, 93, 95, 105, 106
Jain Prākrit, 10
Jāmbavatīvijaya, 118
Jambhaladatta, 93 n. 1
Jānakśharaṇa, 29, 50, 51
Jātakamālā, 83 n. 2, 95
Jātakas, style of, 82, 96, 102
Jayaccandra, of Kanauj, 55
Jayadeva, lyric poet, 113–16
Jayadeva, dramatist, 132
Jayāpīḍa, 117, 123, 125
Jayaratha, 131
Jayasiṁha, of Aṇhilvāḍ, 132
Jayasiṁha, of Kashmir, 54
Jayavallabha, 107, 109
Jinasena, 33
Jinendrabuddhi, 123
Jīvandharacampū, 82
Joel, Rabbi, 106
Jogīmārā inscription, 14
John of Capua, 106
Juvenal, 134
Jyeṣṭhakalaśa, 60

KĀDAMBARĪ, 17, 67, 75–79, 85
Kādambarīkathāsāra, 95
Kālavilāsa, 117
Kalhaṇa, 61–64
Kālidāsa, 12, 13, 15, 16, 17, 19, 22, 26, 29–45, 50, 51, 55, 60, 61, 71, 87, 104, 107, 114, 133
Kalīlah wa Dimnah, 106
Kaliṅgasenā, 90
Kalpanāmaṇḍitikā, 95 n. 6
Kāma, the god, 36
Kāmadeva, 52
Kāmandaki Nītiśāstra, 104
Kāmaśāstra, *Kāmasūtra*, 27, 29, 37, 42, 55, 114, 135
Kamboja, language of, 16
Kaniṣka, 21
Kānti, grace or beauty, 25, 124, 125
Kapphaṇābhyudaya, 56
Kapiñjala, 76
Karaṭaka, 99, 106
Karṇasundarī, 60
Karuṇa, pathetic sentiment, 122
Kashmir, alleged home of Sanskrit, 99; history of, 61–64

Kāśikā Vṛtti, 51
Kāśyapa, 121
Kātantra, 84, 85
Kathā, 68, 69, 73, 75, 81, 84–95, 124, 129
Kathāsaritsāgara, 84
Kātyāyana, 16
Kauṭilya Arthaśāstra, 98
Kavikaṇṭhābharaṇa, 118
Kavīndravacanasamuccaya, 117
Kavirahasya, 18, 53
Kavirāja, title, 26
Kavirāja, author of *Rāghava-Pāṇḍavīya*, 52, 78
Kāvyādarśa, 66, 68, 123–26
Kāvyālaṁkāra, 131
Kāvyamīmāṁsā, 85, 131
Kāvyānuśāsana, 131
Kāvyaprakāśa, 129, 130, 131
Kāvyaprakāśasaṁketa, 131
Khaṇḍanakhaṇḍakhādya, 55
Khāravela, of Kaliṅga, inscription of, 14
Kipling, R., 100
Kirātārjunīya, 48–50
Kosalas, 9
Kṛṣṇa, the god, 114
Kṣemendra, 54, 86, 89, 90, 92, 104, 117, 118
Kubera, the god, 88
Kumāradāsa, 17, 29, 50
Kumāragupta, 57
Kumāralāta, 24, 95 n. 6
Kumārasambhava, 34–37, 48, 50, 56, 104
Kuntaka, Kuntala, 130
Kurukṣetra, 9
Kuru-Pañcālas, 10
Kuṭṭanīmata, 117 n. 1
Kuvalayānanda Kārikās, 132 n. 2

LA FONTAINE, 106
Lakṣaṇā, figurative sense, 128
Lakṣmaṇasena, of Bengal, 16, 108, 113
Lalitāditya, of Kashmir, 52
Lambha, Lambhaka, 90, 124
Lāṭa style, 124 n. 2
Lāvāṇaka, 90
Līlāvatī, 28
Limitations of Sanskrit poetry, 42, 120
Love, 23, 31, 32, 37, 42, 70, 71, 75, 78, 79, 108, 109, 110, 111, 112–15
Lucan, 135
Lucian, 80
Lykophron, 74
Lyly, 74
Lyric poetry, 15, 30–33, 107–20

MADĀLASACAMPŪ, 81
Madanamañcukā, Madanamañjukā, 80, 87, 88, 91, 92
Mādhurya, sweetness, 25, 124, 125
Madiravatī, 92
Māgha, 17, 23, 51, 52, 55, 56, 66, 104 n. 3
Mahābhārata, 11, 23, 25, 51, 53, 83 n. 2, 91, 102
Mahābhāṣya, 96, 99, *and see* Patañjali
Mahākāvya, 123
Māhārāṣṭrī, Prākrit, 13, 15, 20 n. 1, 47, 107
Mahāśvetā, 76, 77
Mahāvīra, language of, 10
Mahiman Bhaṭṭa, 130
Mahimnaḥstava, 119
Mālavikāgnimitra, 29, 30
Malaya, mountain, 56
Mallinātha, 31, 34
Mammaṭa, 35, 43, 126, 129, 130
Man about town, character of, 27, 28
Mānsavega, 87, 91
Mandasor inscription, 29 n. 1, 30, 46, 47
Maṅkha, Maṅkhaka, Maṅkhuka, 54, 132
Māridatta, legend of, 81, 82
Martial, 134
Marvels beyond Thyle, 80
Mātaṅga Divākara, 112
Mayūra, 112
Medhāvin, 123
Meghadūta, 30, 32, 33, 37, 47
Merutuṅga, 135
Metaphors, 44, 64, 72, 124
Metres, 14, 21, 26, 33, 34, 52, 55, 90, 113
Mohamudgara, 112

Mṛcchakaṭikā, 28, 67, 88
Mṛgāṅkadatta, 91
Mṛgāṅkagupta, 60
Muktāphalaketu, 92
Mūlasarvāstivādin school, 88

NĀGĀNANDA, 51, 56
Nāgaraka, 27, 28
Naiṣadhīya, 55
Nalodaya, 55
Nanda, story of, 23
Naravāhanadatta, story of, 80, 87, 95
Nārāyaṇa, 105
Narrative tenses, use of, 16, 103
Nāsik inscription of Siri Pulumāyi, 25
Naṣrallāh ibn Muhammad, 106
Nature, description of, 31, 32, 33, 61, 71, 114
Nāṭyaśāstra, 7, 13, 19, 47, 121, 122, 125, 130, 132
Navasāhasāṅkacarita, 60
Nepal, Brahmanical influence on, 87
Nepalese *Pañcatantra*, 104
Nīlamata Purāṇa, 62
Nītiśāstra, 97
Nītiśataka, 116
Nominal style, 16, 17, 103
North, Sir Thomas, 106
Nyāsa, 123

OḌAYADEVA, 79
Odyssey, 11
Ojas, strength of style, 25, 124
Onion theft, 101

PADALĀLITYA, 72
Padmagupta, 60
Padma Purāṇa, 38 n. 1
Padmāvatī, 92
Pahlavi version of *Pañcatantra*, 98, 106
Paiśācas, 85
Paiśācī Prākrit, 85, 86
Pāli, language, 10 n. 4, 19
Pallavas of Kāñcī, 67
Pañcākhyānaka, 105
Pāñcāla style, 78, 125, 126
Pañcatantra, 84, 86, 98–106
Pāṇini, 7, 8, 9, 10, 11, 12, 13, 16, 18
Pāṇini, poet, 16 n. 2, 118
Parimala, 60
Pariśiṣṭaparvan, 95
Paronomasia, 64, 74, 78 *and see* Śleṣa
Pārśvābhyudaya, 33
Participles, use of, 16, 103
Paruṣā, manner, 126
Pārvatī, 35, 119
Pātālavijaya, 118
Patañjali, 9, 12, 13, 14, 16; and see *Mahābhāṣya*
Pathos, 33, 36, 42, 77, 122
Pattralekhā, 76, 78
Paümacariya, 20 n. 1
Pavanadūta, 33, 113 n. 3
Perfect, 16, 18, 19, 49, 103
Perfect middle, as passive, 17, 34
Periphrastic perfect, 22 n. 1
Petronius, 68
Pforr, A. von, 106
Pilpay, fables of, 106
Piṅgala, 26
Poetics, 121–35
Popular tales, 84–95
Prabandhacintāmaṇi, 135
Prabhākaravardhana, 59
Practice, necessary for poet, 125, 133
Prādyota, 88
Prākrit, 7, 10, 11, 12, 13, 14, 15, 18, 19, 20, 68, 79, 85, 86, 89, 98 n. 3, 124
Prākrit Kāvyas, 14, 47, 52, 56, 107, 124
Prākritisms, in Sanskrit, 18, 19, 89, 105
Prasāda, clearness of style, 25, 124
Pratāparudrayaśobhūṣaṇa, 131
Pratibhā, inspiration, 132
Pratīhārendurāja, 126
Pratiṣṭhāna, 25, 84
Pravarasena, 57, 60; and see *Setubandha*
Prepositional compounds, 17, 34
Preyas, figure, 125, 129
Primary Prākrit, 7
Princes as patrons, 16

Priyaṅgu, story of, 13
Prose, source of, 18; romances, 66–83
Prose and verse narrative style, 83, 95, 102
Puns, *see* Paronomasia *and* Śleṣa
Puṇḍarīka, 76
Pūrṇabhadra, 105
Puṣpadanta, 119

QUALITIES of style, 24, 122, 125, 126, 129, 130; *and see* Gauḍa, Lāṭa, Pāñcāla, Vaidarbha

RĀDHĀ, and Kṛṣṇa, 114, 115
Rāghavapāṇḍavīya, 52
Raghu, 38, 39, 43
Raghuvaṁśa, 22, 31, 37–42, 43, 50
Rākṣasakāvya, 107
Rājaśekhara, 50, 85, 131
Rājataraṅgiṇī, 62–64
Rājyavardhana, 59
Rājyaśrī, 59
Rāma, 40, 41
Rāmāyaṇa, 11, 12, 22, 32, 43, 50, 87
Rāmāyaṇacampū, 82
Rāmāyaṇamañjarī, 54
Rasa, 128; *and see* Sentiment
Rasagaṅgādhara, 130, 131
Rasamañjarī, 131
Rasataraṅgiṇī, 131
Rasavat, figure, 125, 129
Rasika, 134
Rātavarman, 68
Rati, 36, 37
Ratnākara, 53, 54, 119
Ratnaprabhā, 91
Raudra, sentiment of horror, 122
Rāvaṇārjunīya, 18
Refrain, use of, 115
Resignation, 62, 111, 112, 120
Rime, 55, 72, 81, 114, 119
Rīti, style, 125–27
Ṛgveda, 8, 9, 11, 27, 96
Ṛtusaṁhāra, 30, 31, 33, 34, 47
Romances, 66–81
Rudra Bhaṭṭa, 105, 109, 131
Rudradāman, inscription of, 7, 24, 25, 68
Rudraṭa, 105 n. 2, 131
Rūpaka, 122; *and see* Metaphor
Ruyyaka, 131, 132

ŚABDĀLAṀKĀRA, figures of sound, 24, 43
Sabhā, 54
Sādhāraṇadeva, 109
Saduktikarṇāmṛta, 117
Sāhityadarpaṇa, 55, 81
Sahṛdaya, connoisseur, 128, 134
Śaka Satraps, 7
Śaktivega, 90
Śaktiyaśas, 92
Śakuntalā, 30
Samādhi, metaphor, 124
Samasyāpūraṇa, 33, 135
Samayamātṛkā, 117
Śambhalīmata, 117
Śambhu, 109
Sameness, of style, 125
Saṁgati, poetic convention, 133
Saṁhitās, language of the, 8, 9
Sāṁkhya-Yoga, 22, 42
Samudrabandhu, 132
Samudragupta, 16, 26, 30, 43
Śaṅkara, 112, 119
Śaṅkuka, 130
Sanskrit, 7–20, 84, 97, 99, 124
Śānta, sentiment of resignation, 122
Śāntiśataka, 112
Śaptaśataka, 109–11
Śaraṇa, 113
Sarasvatī, sacrifice, 9
Sarasvatīkaṇṭhābharaṇa, 118, 131
Sargabandha, 123, 124
Śārṅgadhara, 117
Śarvavarman, 84, 85
Śaśāṅkavatī, 91
Sātavāhana, 47, 60, 84, 107; *and see* Hāla
Sāttvika, feelings, 122
Satyra, of Petronius, 68
Saundarananda, 23
Śaurasenī Prākrit, 13
Schiller, 33
Seasons, 31, 32
Semonides, 116

Sentiments, 25, 42, 115, 125, 126, 128, 129, 130, 131, 133
Setubandha, 47, 56, 57
Śibi, legend of, 100
Siddharṣi, 15
Śīghrakavi, Śīghrakavitā, 16, 135
Śīlābhaṭṭārikā, 78
Śilahāra, 61
Śilhaṇa, 112
Siṁhāsanadvātriṁśikā, 94
Similes, 44, 45, 64, 72, 135
Simplicity of style, 24, 126
Sindhurāja, 60
Śiṣṭas, language of, 12, 13
Śiśupālavadha, 51, 52
Sītā, 40, 41
Sītābengā inscription, 14
Śiva, 35, 36, 37, 42, 48, 49, 53, 54
Śivadāsa, 93
Śivasvāmin, 56
Skandagupta, 30
Śleṣa, double entendre, 26, 45; firm structure, 124
Ślokasaṁgraha, see *Bṛhatkathāślokasaṁgraha*
Śobhā, charm, 125
Soma, father of Vāgbhaṭa, 132
Somadeva, 86, 89–92, 104
Somadeva, author of *Yaśastilaka*, 81
Southern Pañcatantra, 104
Southern style, *see* Vaidarbha
Sphoṭa, 127
Śṛṅgāra, erotic sentiment, 122
Śṛṅgāraprakāśa, 56 n. 2, 113 n. 1, 118
Śṛṅgāraśataka, 111
Śṛṅgāratilaka, 107; by Rudra, 109, 131
Śrīdhara, 28 n. 4
Śrīdharadāsa, 117
Śrīdharasena, 50
Śrī-Harṣa, 17, 55
Śrīkaṇṭhacarita, 54
Sthaviras, Paiśācī of, 86
Sthāyibhāva, abiding emotions, 121
Strength, of style, 25, 124, 126
Study, necessary for poet, 125
Style, of Aśvaghoṣa, 23, 24; of Kālidāsa, 37, 43–45; of Bhāravi, 49, 51; of Kumāradāsa, 50; of Māgha, 52; of Vākpati, 52; of Bāṇa, 58, 59, 78, 79; of Bilhaṇa, 61; of Kalhaṇa, 64; of Daṇḍin, 71, 72; of Subandhu, 73, 74; of Budhasvāmin, 89; of Somadeva, 89; of *Tantrākhyāyika*, 102, 103; of Amaru, 109, 110; of Bhartṛhari, 111; of Jayadeva, 114, 115
Subandhu, 18, 25, 70, 71, 72–75, 78, 82, 85
Subhāṣitāvali, 117, 134
Sudatta, 81
Śūdraka, 75, 77
Suggestion, in poetry, 33, 37, 109, 115, 126–31
Śukanāsa, 75
Sukumāratā, gentleness of style, 124
Sumanottarā, tale of 13
Sundarī, story of, 23
Suprabhadeva, 51
Surāṣṭras, language of, 16
Suratamañjarī, 92
Sūryaprabha, 91
Sūryaśataka, 112
Sūtrālaṁkāra, 24, 95
Svayaṁvara, 38
Sweetness, of style, 25, 124, 126
Syriac versions of *Pañcatantra*, 106

TANTRĀKHYĀYIKA, 84, 98–104. 105, 106
Tārāpīḍa, 75, 77
Tennyson, and Kālidāsa, 30, 31
Textus ornatior of *Pañcatantra*, 105; *simplicior*, 105.
Theories of poetics, 121–35
Threefold division of poetry, 128
Thukydides, 33, 63
Tilakamañjarī, 79, 95
Tone, Dhvani, 127–30
Translation, alleged, of epics from Prākrit, 7, 11, 12
Translations of the *Pañcatantra*, 106
Tripur

Triśatī, 28 n. 4
Trivikrama Bhaṭṭa, 80, 81
Tupper, Martin, 116
Turuṣka kings, 62

UDĀRATVA, elevation, 25, 124
Udayana, 88
Udbhaṭa, 123, 126
Uddīpana, factors which enflame emotion, 121
Uddyotakara, 72, 123
Umāpatidhara, 113
Upamā, simile, 122
Upamitibhavaprapañcakathā, 15
Upanāgarikā, manner, 126
Upaniṣads, language of, 8
Ūrjasvin, figure, 125, 129

VĀGBHAṬA, 132, 134
Vāgbhaṭālaṁkāra, 132
Vaidarbha style, 25, 26, 43, 46, 47, 51, 61, 67, 71, 124, 125
Vairāgyaśataka, 111, 112
Vaiśampāyana, 75, 76
Vajjālagga, 107, 109
Vākpati, 52, 82
Vakrokti, metaphorical expression, 78, 125, 126
Vakroktijīvita, 130
Vakroktipañcāśikā, 119
Vākyapadīya, 111, 123
Vallabhadeva, 34
Vālmīki, 12, 32, 41; and see *Rāmāyaṇa*
Vāmana, 55, 125, 126, 127
Varāhamihira, 28
Vararuci, 14, 121
Varmalāta, 51
Vāsavadattā, story of, 13
Vāsavadattā, 60, 73–79
Vastu, subject matter, 128
Vasubandhu, 29 n. 1
Vāsudeva, 55
Vatsabhaṭṭi, 30, 46
Vātsyāyana, 27, 135; and see *Kāmaśāstra*
Vaṭudāsa, 117
Vedic language, 7–10
Velā, 91
Vernaculars, 15 n. 2, 20, 28, 105, 106
Vetālapañcaviṁśatikā, 91, 93, 94
Vibhāvas, factors, 121
Vicchitti, charm, 18, 132
Videhas, 9
Vidyādhara, author, 130, 133
Vidyādharas, 87, 90, 91
Vidyānātha, 131, 133
Vikramāditya, 30, 92, 107, 109, 113
Vikramāditya VI, of Kalyāṇa, 60, 61
Vikramāṅkadevacarita, 60, 113
Vimalasūri, 20 n. 1
Vīra, heroic sentiment, 122
Vīrasena, inscription of, 26
Vīreśvara, 109
Virgil, 43
Viṣamaśīla, 92
Viṣṇu, 42
Viṣṇuśarman, 98
Viśvanātha, 35, 129, 130
Vṛtti, manner, 126
Vyabhicāri-bhāva, transient emotions, 121
Vyaktiviveka, 130
Vyañjanā, suggestion, 127

WESTERN style, *see* Vaidarbha
White Island, legend of, 91
Wonder, sentiment of, 42, 75, 122
Word order, in prose, 18

XENOPHON, of Ephesos, 80

YAKṢA, 32
Yamaka, 43, 55, 56, 114, 122
Yaśastilaka, 81, 82, 95
Yāska, 16
Yaśodharman, 29 n. 1
Yaśovarman, 16, 52
Yātrās, 113
Yaugandharāyaṇa, 88
Yavakrīta, story of, 13
Yavanas, 80; perhaps Muhammadans, 116
Yayāti, story of, 13
Yoga philosophy, 42